A Visual Artist's Guide to Estate Planning

Based on a Conference Co-Sponsored by

The Marie Walsh Sharpe Art Foundation and

The Judith Rothschild Foundation

Part I
Prepared by:

Wolf, Keens & Company, Inc.
200 North Little Falls St., Suite 303
Falls Church, VA 22046
Project Director: William Keens
Project Coordinator: Anne Watson

Part II
Editor: Barbara Hoffman, Esq., Chair, Committee on Art Law, Association of the Bar of the City of New York

Book and Cover Design by Catherine Sandler

Printing by McCormick-Armstrong/Williams Division, L.L.C.

Library of Congress Catalog Card Number: 98-61019

ISBN 0-9665188-0-2

TABLE OF CONTENTS

Can I give my work to a museum?
What should I do with my papers?

FORWARD

No one likes to think about death. Artists are no different in this regard. Many of us have put off making a will. But we have to think about the acres of objects, made by our own hands, which will be our legacy. As Cynthia Carlson said, "If you don't make a plan, someone else will do it for you."

Although an artist's estate may contain assets other than art, it is the art that concerns many of us most. Planning for the care, storage, possible sale, or other disposition of our work after we die is a large part of an artist's estate planning.

On April 4 and 5, 1997, artists, lawyers, accountants, dealers, and others in the arts met at Philip Pearlstein's loft in Manhattan. The conference was a culmination of discussions which began in 1990.

A Visual Artist's Guide to Estate Planning is the record of our conference. We intend this book to help you ask the right questions and seek the appropriate advisors, whether you are a poor, neither rich nor poor, or rich artist. We hope that reading about the experiences of other artists will help you clarify your thoughts. Part II contains additional information prepared under the auspices of the Association of the Bar of the City of New York Committee on Art Law on estate planning and administration matters.

This publication is distributed with the understanding that The Marie Walsh Sharpe Art Foundation, The Judith Rothschild Foundation, and the Association of the Bar of the City of New York are not engaged in rendering legal, accounting, or other professional service in this book. If legal or accounting advice or other expert assistance is required, the services of a competent professional person should be sought. Further, the views expressed in Part I are the personal expressions of the individual participants at the conference and not necessarily those of The Marie Walsh Sharpe Art Foundation, The Judith Rothschild Foundation, or the Association of the Bar of the City of New York.

In the past few years the entire structure of support for the arts and for artists has gone through dramatic changes. With the diminishing involvement of the public sector at all levels, artists have increasingly had to rely on the relatively small number of private sponsors willing to step into the breach. Rare among such entities, The Marie Walsh Sharpe Art Foundation was organized around the principle that artists know best what artists require to pursue their creative direction, and understand best how those requirements may change over time.

The result has been a close, amicable, and fruitful collaboration between the officers of the Foundation and an Artists Advisory Committee composed of practicing artists and colleagues closely involved with the contemporary arts scene. At every stage this board has set the course not only with the aim of initiating specific programs, but with the hope of stimulating discussion within the larger community of funders about how to proceed in meeting the ever more complex demands facing artists in this country. To that end, The Marie Walsh Sharpe Art Foundation has engaged in ongoing dialogue with numerous groups in the field as well as with artists and experts eager to cooperate in addressing these issues.

This is our second publication. The first, *Roundtable Discussion on the Needs of Visual Artists,* was the record of a conference of thirty artists, called by The Marie Walsh Sharpe Art Foundation in November of 1988.

The Artists Advisory Committee, appointed by the Foundation after the 1988 conference, initiated and developed The Space Program and the Hotline. The Space Program awards free studios in New York City to artists and the Hotline answers questions on a host of topics which concern visual artists. A consortium of art foundations now funds the Hotline.

Joyce E. Robinson and Charles J. Hemmingsen, the principal officers of the Foundation, administer all the programs with the assistance of Kim Taylor and Nan Tirado. The Foundation is based in Colorado Springs, Colorado.

We wish to thank Harvey S. Shipley Miller, John James Oddy, and The Judith Rothschild Foundation for their generous contribution to the Estate Planning for Visual Artists project.

We would also like to thank Barbara Hoffman, Chair, and The Committee on Art Law of the Association of the Bar of the City of New York, for their contributions of effort, time, and expertise in developing Part II of this publication.

Please pass this along to another artist. Let us know if and how this publication has helped you.

Cynthia Carlson

Chuck Close

Janet Fish

Philip Pearlstein

Irving Sandler

Harriet Shorr

Robert Storr

Left to Right
Chuck Close, Irving Sandler, Robert Storr
Facilitators of the Visual Artists Estate Planning Conference

INTRODUCTION

Dead artists leave two bodies, their own, and a body of work.
 —Harriet Shorr, Artist

An elderly artist, named Turku Trajan, spent winters working as a short-order cook and sold his paintings on cardboard at the summer art fair in Greenwich Village....
 My friends and I walked into an enormous loft, jammed to the ceiling with towering heroic figures and angels with wings. They were visionary, not academic; eccentric but beautiful. A narrow pathway led to a small room where the artist was working on a smaller figure. Several years later he died, without heirs, as far as I know. The dealer, Virginia Zabriskie, acquired the estate in 1964, but in the thirty-three years since, has not been able to sell a piece or even give one away.
 Variations of this story are playing out constantly across the country, with or without families participating. This country has produced thousands of serious artists, many of whom have occasionally exhibited and sold some works, but despite seriousness and talent, never became prominent. The art departments of our colleges are staffed by many such artists.
 What becomes of the art they have produced when they die? It is easy to say an artist's heirs will just sell some work to pay estate taxes, but it cannot be overlooked that the reason there is so much work on hand is that the artist's works have not found a market to begin with. Logic never enters into the making of art in our society.
 —Philip Pearlstein, Artist

Death in the art world is going to be a huge industry very soon. This goes well beyond major artists with highly successful careers and highly marketable works. Every block in SoHo and Tribeca has more artists living in it than lived in this entire city in the fifties. There is a vast inventory of material to be dealt with.
 —Alan Schwartzman, Writer

On April 4 and 5, 1997, The Marie Walsh Sharpe Art Foundation and The Judith Rothschild Foundation convened a conference to discuss practical and legal issues related to artists' estates in planning and in the administration of the estate after the artist's death. The idea for the gathering originated with artists on the Artists Advisory Committee of The Marie Walsh Sharpe Art Foundation: Cynthia Carlson, Chuck Close, Janet Fish, Philip Pearlstein, Harriet Shorr, and Robert Storr, and Irving Sandler, chair. At a previous roundtable on the needs of visual artists, the Artists Advisory Committee identified the topic of estate planning as significant enough for a roundtable of its own. As Irving Sandler said, "sensitive to the needs of the art community, we recognized the growing concern that artists had with estate planning—the bewilderment, the frustration. We hoped that we could help in this matter." Sandler approached The Judith Rothschild Foundation which, because of its related mission, formed a partnership with The Marie Walsh Sharpe Art Foundation to support the project. Artists, accountants, archivists, attorneys, curators, dealers, writers, and representatives from foundations, government, museums, and other nonprofit organizations were invited to meet to discuss the particular problems faced by visual artists in planning their estates, and the financial burdens placed on an estate by a body of art work. Sandler stated that "the purpose of the roundtable was to walk an artist through the problems of estate planning."

For some time prior to the conference, the Committee on Art Law of the Association of the Bar of the City of New York had been planning the publication of a book for visual artists to address their special estate planning and administration needs, and welcomed involving its members in the conference. One result of the collaboration between The Marie Walsh Sharpe Art Foundation, The Judith Rothschild Foundation, and the Association of the Bar of the City of New York Committee on Art Law is this publication. This publication has two main parts, as well as a glossary, an appendix of forms, and a list of resources. Using a question-and-answer format, Part I introduces general estate planning concepts and offers a practical and general legal discussion of the issues raised at the conference. Part II consists of a more in-depth discussion of policy, ethics, and law on selected estate planning and administration issues for visual artists, authored primarily by members of the subcommittee of Artists and Taxes of the Committee on Art Law of the Association of the Bar of the City of New York.

No two artists' estates are alike, and no two estate plans will be the same. But, whether they know it or not, all artists have an estate plan: if you die without a will, state law determines your estate plan for you. This publication is a guide to the process of estate planning and administration. While this publication covers all facets of estate planning and the important highlights of estate administration, it is not a substitute for competent legal advice. In it, you will find suggestions on how to select a legal advisor and other members of your estate planning and administration team.

Not only the seriously ill or the financially successful artist should consider an estate plan. Even if you have few assets, a carefully planned estate can help insure that your work and ideas will continue to be presented as you wish. If you leave no instructions about what to do with your work, it might not receive the recognition it would otherwise. Moreover, it might place a huge time and financial burden on surviving family and friends. Estate planning involves more than simply writing a will. For a visual artist, the process of estate planning—setting priorities, making an inventory, choosing an attorney, choosing an executor, choosing an accountant, and articulating plans for the disposition of your artwork—can help insure the continued life of your work and ideas.

Left to Right
Harriet Shorr, Cynthia Carlson, Kate Horsfield

SETTING PRIORITIES

As artists who have a certain amount of recognition but not a great deal, I think we have a different perspective. It seems to us that there are two things to be concerned about: the well-being of the person to whom you give the property, and the well-being of the property itself. We need to think through these kinds of claims and find some way to make them harmonize.
   —Betty Woodman, Artist

Three things are important. First, having clarity of purpose: you have to know who you are giving your work to and what their intent will be. No person that you leave in control will have the same agenda as you do. You are starting a process that is out of your control. Second, the choice of who to leave works to. Finally, intellectual property: what artists really have is a spirit and a philosophy—intangible things put in the material fact of the objects they make. There are laws and decisions to protect that. The use of copyright and reproductions is one example, and should be stated. If you put images of works on a CD-ROM, you should think about what will be done with that. Will it show up in thirty years in a Nike commercial?
   —Peter Stevens, Artist

Why do I need a will?

My partner of fourteen years died suddenly at the age of thirty-nine. She died without a will, but she had very definite ideas about what she wanted to happen to her work. When she died, her estate was settled in Illinois. In that state, if there is no will, the estate is divided among the primary family members. One-third went to each of her parents, and to her brother. She had always had a very problematic relationship with her brother and his acquisition of one third of her estate was extremely painful for all of us who knew how passionate she was about everything, and how much she would have disliked her brother's inheritance of her possessions.
   —Kate Horsfield, Video Data Bank

A will is a legal declaration by which you dispose of your property. It takes effect on death and disposes only of the property you own at the

Left to Right
Nancy Fried, Philip Pearlstein

time of death. If you die without a valid will, you are said to have died "intestate," and the laws of the state where you lived govern the distribution of your property. Generally speaking, property goes to relatives: first, spouse and children; then parents and siblings; then other relatives. (Gay and lesbian partners have no automatic rights to inherit property if you die without a written will.) Even if these state-designated heirs want to care for your work and your reputation, they may have little understanding of your career or how the art world operates. If you die without a will, you also lose the ability to choose who will administer your estate.

Therefore, if you have specific wishes for the disposition of your art or other property, you need to make a will. Since each state has its own conditions for properly executing a will, legal advice from an attorney is strongly recommended. An attorney can also help you focus your priorities and establish an estate plan that meets your goals, whether to provide bequests for friends and family, to avoid estate tax liability, or to establish a charitable foundation to promote your ideas and values. Before visiting an attorney, however, it is important to think about your goals for your estate.

What should be done with my art work?

When I die, my studio will have to be emptied of all my paintings and toys. At least I won't have to do the work. But once the stuff is in the moving van, where will it go? After all these years of painting, have I simply created a terrible burden for my wife and children? They will have to give directions to the driver of that van. It almost seems that the easiest solution would be for them to take a few souvenirs and have the rest driven to the town dump.
  —Philip Pearlstein, Artist

I represent a man whose brother was an artist. He asked me to help circulate his brother's work, which is stored in a garage. He suffers great pain because he knows that when he dies there will be no one to take care of his brother's work. He would have been pleased to have had his brother's permission to destroy some of it.
  —David Brown, Attorney

Left to Right
David Brown, Janet Fish, Beverly Wolff, Stephen Weil

Storage, conservation, and cataloging needs create special problems for the visual artist's estate. It is important to separate artistic property from other physical possessions.
—Barbara Hoffman, Attorney

The David Smith estate decided not to make duplicates of the sculptures. Other estates have made other decisions when artists leave no instructions. A sculpture executed by the heirs according to the instructions of the artist is considered an authentic sculpture. Something made by the heirs on their own is not necessarily accorded the same value. Leave detailed instructions.
—Andre Emmerich, Dealer

Copyright needs to be specified carefully in your will. Artists' heirs abuse this a lot. Their works of art wind up on coffee mugs or jigsaw puzzles. It is important to anticipate what kinds of usage you want for your art.
—Beverly Wolff, Attorney

How do you want your work to be preserved and presented? Is continued exhibition of your work a top priority? Do you want your work to be distributed to your family and friends? Do you want to donate your work to a public, nonprofit organization, such as a museum, art center, university gallery, library, historical society, hospital, or school?

Do you want your work sold or reproduced to provide income? If you are a sculptor, do you want to authorize further editions of reproductions to be manufactured after your death? At what scale? If you are a photographer, do you want to authorize reprints from your negatives? On a greeting card? For digital distribution? If you are a performance artist, do you want the videos of your performances to be shown? Do you want works on consignment to galleries or on loan to museums to remain there after your death? If your work can produce income, should the focus be on short-term or long-term gains?

Where should your art be stored? Do you want it to be collected and maintained in one place? What financial resources will be available to pay for storage or other expenses of caring for the artwork? Can you afford a life insurance policy to pay for storage of your art after your death? (See Part II, page 71 for more information on insurance.)

Left to Right
Allan Schwartzman, Betty Woodman, Cesar Trasobares, Scott Hoot

You must decide what you want done with your artwork, and the intangible intellectual property rights to those works, which can be transferred separately. An important asset of your artistic estate may be the potential of these intellectual property rights, particularly the copyright interests, in your work. Should your estate manage your copyrights, or should they be transferred with the work? Disposition of and control of copyrights raises issues of tax, artistic control, and valuation. (See Part II, page 96 for more information on copyright.) If you do not specify what you want done, those who inherit your work will make those decisions for you.

Who should benefit from my estate?

The family tends to treat the work with the same attitude they had toward the work when the artist was alive, which isn't always friendly.
—*Janet Fish, Artist*

Most artists have not thought about their estates at all. It is amazing to devote your whole life to a body of work and then just assume it will find its way into institutions and the hands of those people whom you would choose.
—*Cesar Trasobares, Estate Project for Artists with AIDS*

One purpose of the estate plan is to take care of the heirs. The artist has to make some decisions. When an artist does a will, Who gets what? Who will own the body of work?
—*Gilbert S. Edelson, Attorney*

Do you want to leave your work to a spouse, partner, or children? Do they want the responsibility of taking care of your art works? Talk to the people or organizations you want to benefit from your estate. Do not surprise them—make sure they know what you would like done. For example, unnegotiated gifts to museums or other institutions could be refused, leaving the work in limbo.

Adrian Piper

What is important to save?

I am an only child and the only executor of my mother's estate. Going through her estate, I discovered that she had saved everything I had ever done, written, drawn, or played with. So I have a complete record! I have also had to deal with her estate more generally, and have discovered it is difficult, because almost everything has sentimental value. I found it extremely difficult to throw anything away. My problem is that I only have a few more decades on the planet, and there's a lot I want to do. I don't have time to spend the rest of my life dealing with work I've already done.
  —Adrian Piper, Artist

Don't throw it out. Artists should save letters, catalogs, photos, invitations, and personal writings—anything that will help others understand the texture of the art. Imagine what would be relevant to someone in the future who wants to write a catalog or biography.
  —Avis Berman, Art historian

Keep records of business relationships, and a folder of contracts.
  —David Brown, Attorney

In your studio, what is art and what isn't? By what works do you want to be represented? Who should have access to what materials? In most cases, competing benefits must be weighed; there will be trade-offs. Is placement more or less important than income? Is it more important to preserve art objects and other contributions to the field, such as videotapes or correspondence, or to minimize the volume of material that will have to be dealt with after your death?

Photographs, journals, gallery announcements, critical reviews, or works in progress can give scholars and art historians materials they need to evaluate your career, but the family or friends who come to close up your studio could have a difficult time throwing anything away. Organizing your materials will make it easier for them to carry out your wishes for your work. If you are concerned about privacy, you can restrict access to certain materials—for example, you may choose to restrict access to a diary while the people mentioned in it are still alive. Art historians, scholars, and curators, however, urge artists to be generous in granting access and to not censor materials.

*Left to Right
Betty Cuningham, Richard Shebairo, Roger Anthony*

CREATING AN ART INVENTORY

Artists, while they are alive, should make some kind of inventory or listing of what's what, so this doesn't leave painful decisions for people who care about the work for more than commercial reasons and want to see it keep its integrity.
   —*Cynthia Carlson, Artist*

Worry about inventory before worrying about storage. That way, the heirs will know what needs they will have for storage. The most effective approach for making an initial inventory is simply to start at one location (building, floor, room, closet) and list every item before moving on to the next.
   —*Roger Anthony, The DeKooning Conservatorship*

Generally, working is considered life-affirming. Doing an inventory is not.
   —*Scott Hoot, Volunteer Lawyers for the Arts, Artist Legacy Project*

I have begun a complete inventory of my own work. I hired a graduate student in philosophy. Philosophy graduate students are very good on computers, they are scrupulous, they are careful and analytical, good with detail. And they are smart. This student is working on FoxPro, which is an inventory system for the Macintosh. I pay him $10 an hour. He is cataloging everything I have ever done. When he completes this process, he will match up each item on the inventory with slide reproductions, transparencies, photographs, to see if there is anything that remains undocumented. I like the idea of putting things on CD-ROM.
   —*Adrian Piper, Artist*

It is a matter of information, because you cannot save every little object. The idea of putting things on disk—some organization should start thinking about it. It's an interesting way to preserve this kind of information, because then you can cross-reference it and you don't have the burden of all the objects.
   —*Joan Jonas, Artist*

Preparing an inventory is onerous, but it is not just for the IRS. It also helps living artists keep track of their work.
—*Avis Berman, Art Historian*

After thinking about your priorities, the time comes to create an inventory— a record of the existence of your work. Doing so not only will help someone mounting an exhibition to assemble pieces of your work, but also will help scholars and art historians understand the development of your career.

What should an inventory of art include?

An art inventory should list all your works of art, noting the location (in the studio, on exhibition, on loan, on consignment, in private collections), with the dimensions, date, title, medium, or other descriptive information. You will also want to specify which works are finished, which are works-in-progress, and which are preparatory studies or were never intended for public viewing or sale. Even if your work has not enjoyed commercial success, a complete inventory of your work will help determine the monetary value of your artistic estate.

The inventory should include information on installation and maintenance, ownership, and exhibition records, your writings (diaries, journals, instructions on installations, articles), writing by others about you (monographs, catalogs, articles), videotapes or CD-ROMs of your work, and intangible assets such as copyrights, trademarks, and other intellectual property. It is useful to keep a record of all your contracts and any special business relationships as well. (See Appendix A for sample inventory worksheets.)

CHOOSING AN ATTORNEY

You can go to a lawyer who belongs to a prestigious law firm and has a lot of experience in estate planning, but who doesn't know how the art world works. There is a limit to the advice this person can give you.
  —Hermine Ford, Artist

More than worrying about whether a lawyer specializes in art, ask if there is respect and passion for preservation of those values that the artist wants to maintain.
  —Peter Stevens, Artist

You want someone who is knowledgeable, who specializes in estate planning, who is knowledgeable about you. You must trust them. Artists who cannot afford a lawyer can consult Volunteer Lawyers for the Arts.
  —Gilbert S. Edelson, Attorney

The artist had been represented by an attorney who was reputable and respected in the art world, who also represented the artist's gallery. When there were questions about what works were inventoried and what works were not, the attorney advised us that it was appropriate for him to be representing both the artist and the gallery. This became problematic when disputes arose.
  —Alan Schwartzman, Writer

Ultimately, the lawyer does what you want. You need a well-thought-out plan. The lawyer will explain the problems with it.
  —Richard Shebairo, C.P.A., P.C.

Estate planning involves much more than drafting a will and good estate planning for artists requires a variety of skills. Ideally, the attorney who draws up your will and helps plan your estate is someone you trust, who is familiar with your work, who is knowledgeable about the art world as well as the law of trusts and estates. This particular combination of skills and experience may not be easy to find; you must decide which qualities are most important for your situation. An arts lawyer by definition is

Left to Right
Joan Jonas, Philip Pearlstein, Gil Edelson, Charles Bergman

engaged in the practice of overlapping legal disciplines—copyright, trusts and estates, commercial transactions. Therefore, the approach and recommendations of an arts lawyer may be different from those of a trusts and estates lawyer.

How do I find a lawyer who has experience in dealing with artists' estates and estate planning for artists?

Ask fellow artists, your accountant, or your dealer, if you have one, for recommendations. If you do not currently have a lawyer, interview several attorneys before choosing one. Be sure to discuss price and find out what services will be provided for the price. Make sure the attorney has the expertise you require and that you feel confident with his or her answers. If the attorney is willing to accept art for payment, establish the value of the attorney's services prior to any exchange of art.

In addition to being satisfied with the attorney's competence as an estate planner, you must find the fee arrangements acceptable. The question of fees should be raised at the earliest possible moment; for instance, in the telephone call making the initial appointment. Will that first visit result in a fee even if the attorney is not the one you use for the estate plan? Will the fee be based only on time spent, or is there a maximum? If the fee is a fixed amount, how many drafts or rewrites are possible? What eventualities will change the fee estimate or fixed amount? What disbursements will be charged to the artist?

In addition to the estate planning fee now, you should find out on what fee basis the attorney or law firm will do the legal work needed to administer the estate. There is no requirement that the executor employ the lawyer who drafted the will. Therefore an agreement to reduce the estate planning fees in exchange for being the estate's attorney restricts the executor's discretion and may lead to a difficult working relationship between them.

What should I talk about with an attorney?

There is no single answer, no uniform estate plan for any artist. There is a menu of things that can be done. It depends on individual circumstances. Test an idea. Will it work? What is the downside?
—*Gilbert S. Edelson, Attorney*

Don't be afraid to ask, How much is the estate plan going to cost me?
—*Erik Stapper, Attorney*

In the process of designing an estate plan, a great deal of factual information must be gathered and communicated to your attorney. In addition to creating the inventory of your art and archival material, you will need to collect and organize family information; financial information, including an inventory of assets; and your "dispositive wishes" (where you want your assets to go). Complete, accurate financial information is required in order to create an effective plan for any estate taxes and the administration of your estate. Assets can be tangible or intangible. Tangible assets include, for example, cash, bank accounts, furniture, book and magazine collections, real estate (buildings, land), securities (stocks, bonds, other investments), or life insurance. Intangible assets include copyright, trademark, and other intellectual property.

Estate planning requires collaboration. You must feel comfortable with your attorney, whomever you choose. Once you have made your choice, make your attorney aware of your concerns—are you most interested in providing income for your family, avoiding estate taxes, or making sure your work remains in the public eye? Do you want a charitable trust or a private foundation created? What disposition will be made of your artwork? (See Part II, pages 61–67, 87–95 for more information on trusts and foundations.)

Do not hesitate to ask questions about the benefits and drawbacks of what you want, or to suggest that your attorney seek advice on issues particular to artists' estates, such as copyright and valuation of art works, if he or she is not familiar with the art world or more sophisticated tax planning techniques. You may also want to talk to your attorney about a health care proxy and a durable power of attorney. (See Appendices I–O for sample forms.)

Your attorney will provide legal advice, but he or she will be carrying out your decisions, so you need to be clear about what you want and to communicate your wishes effectively.

CHOOSING AN EXECUTOR

Should I name my gallery as my executor? How do I know if these people will be there in five or twenty years, and how do I know if I will still be with them?
  —*Nancy Fried, Artist*

I am a painter; my mother was a painter; my husband is a painter; and my daughter is a painter. I don't know what kind of burden we are leaving to the next generation. When my mother died, we had no idea what we were getting into. She had asked an aunt of mine to be the executor. My aunt was ready to put all her work out onto the street to save $125 a month in rent for an apartment on the Upper West Side.
  —*Emily Mason, Artist*

Choose someone with the most amount of expertise and the least amount of vested self-interest.
  —*Peter Stevens, Artist*

Pick an executor you trust, and trust them to get advice. There should be no surprises. Talk to them in advance. Trust them, because things change. You have to give your executor a certain amount of discretion, based on your stated intent.
  —*Gilbert S. Edelson, Attorney*

Control becomes an emotional issue when partners, spouses, and family members are the only ones in charge.
  —*Bill Jensen, Artist*

Left to Right
Harvey S. Shipley Miller, Barbara Hoffman, Elizabeth Catlett, Fred Lazarus

Knowledge of financial matters is not necessarily the most important qualification of an executor. Personal integrity, devotion to duty, and competence must be paramount.

Don't ignore the psychological impact of failing to choose a loved family member as an executor. Competent professionals can always be hired by the executor.

—Barbara Hoffman, Attorney

Although the duties, responsibilities, and even title of the person who administers an estate vary depending on state law, this publication uses the term executor to refer generically to such a person. <u>The fundamental duty of the executor is loyalty to the beneficiaries of the estate.</u> Above all, make your executor and any advisors aware of your priorities, choose people who are knowledgeable about the art world and sympathetic to your work, and encourage them to seek advice from other experts whenever necessary.

What does an executor do?

If there are assets to be sold, the executor has to sell them. If your estate is owed money, the executor must collect it. The executor may have to pay funeral expenses, other bills, and income or estate taxes, to inventory the art (if you have not done so), or to file insurance claims. The executor follows the instructions in your will and distributes the property in accordance with your wishes. The executor also chooses an attorney (who may or may not be the same person who wrote your will) to handle legal issues, and an appraiser to appraise your artwork.

The final task of an executor is the accounting, the procedure by which the executor turns the assets over to the beneficiaries. The executor must be able to show that the estate tax returns were accurate and fair; the heirs may sue the executor for liability. An executor's job usually lasts three to four years, but may last considerably longer if there are assets to dispose of or manage, such as copyright interests. (See Part II, page 81 for the Executor's or Administrator's Checklist.)

Left to Right
Stephen Weil, André Emmerich

Who can be an executor?

An executor should be someone who is going to protect the things you are most interested in.
   —Betty Cuningham, Dealer

From an artist's point of view, dealers are not disinterested. Many artists' estates and families have had poor experiences using a dealer as executor.
   —Harriet Shorr, Artist

Make sure that the person you ask to serve knows what they are getting into, how much work is involved in administering an estate.
   —Cynthia Carlson, Artist

We have separated the role of the executor and the role of the ultimate beneficiary or trustee—often they are filled by the same person.
   —Fred Lazarus, President, Maryland College of Art

Executors have to be careful, especially if there is contention with the heirs. It can be avoided with the proper will.
   —Stephen E. Weil, Attorney

You can appoint anyone as your executor. Ideally, the executor should be trustworthy, knowledgeable about the art world, and committed to maintaining or enhancing your reputation as an artist. Since the executor must manage your estate, you may want to look for someone who is well organized, or it may be more important to you that the executor is someone who is passionate about your art. Make sure the person understands the amount of work required. If your executor does not have much experience in dealing with the art world, you can select a group of advisors to help your executor—people with expertise who might not have time to be executors themselves. However, it is the executor who has final authority and, unless written in the will, the group of advisors has no "official status."

It is extremely important to name a competent successor to the original executor, especially if the original executor is someone close to your age or in poor health. This can have a significant effect on whether or not your wishes are carried out. (See Part II, page 81 for more information on executors.)

Whomever you choose as your executor, consider any possible draw-backs or conflicts of interest. An executor should be someone who will act in the best interests of your estate, not someone who might adminis-ter your estate for his or her own benefit. Your executor will be making decisions that require balancing the competing demands of emotion and money, speed of sale and maximum price. Any choice has both advan-tages and drawbacks.

Attorney as executor. Since an estate can be planned to maximize or minimize an executor's commission, the choice of the attorney who planned the estate to also administer the estate could create a con-flict of interest. In addition, the administration of an estate by the executor can be managed to either maximize or minimize associated legal fees. When acting in both capacities, some attorneys are willing to waive the executor's commission if they also serve as the lawyer for the estate.

Accountant as executor. Accountants may have the tax and financial experience, and level of professional integrity to fill the role of execu-tor. Keep this in mind as the relationship with your accountant devel-ops. Expose them to the broad picture, both family and financial. Evaluate whether they have the depth of character and sensitivity to your particular situation to carry out the intent, as well as the instruc-tions, of your will: for your artwork, and for your heirs.

Dealer as executor. Some dealers are reluctant to serve as executors as there is the potential for a conflict of interest between their role as dealer and as executor. Since an artistic estate could be managed in such a way as to maximize the commissions a dealer would receive from work sold, a dealer named as executor may want each decision reviewed by a court, which could lead to delays. Many dealers prefer to act in an advisory capacity to the executor.

Spouse, family member, or friend as executor. Often the executor is a surviving partner, spouse, child, or other relative or friend.

Sometimes artists do not want to burden their families; they just want them to benefit from the estate. Talk to your beneficiaries; some may want the responsibility of placing your art works according to your wishes, some may not (especially if they are artists as well and must contend with their own art works). It is also important to consider the possible personal and emotional effect on family relationships if, in the interest of efficiency, only one family member is named as executor and the surviving spouse is relegated to the role of beneficiary.

Multiple executors. It may be more efficient to name one executor, but it is possible to name co-executors or to divide your estate into different areas. You could name one executor for your art and another for papers of historical and cultural value, for example. Or, you could designate artistic or literary advisors to assist your executor. In any of these scenarios, personal relations and dynamics should be taken into account. Keep in mind, executors are paid from the estate, unless they are willing to waive their fees. (See Part II, page 116 for more information on conflicts of interest.)

What do I tell my executor?

In the Warhol estate, snapshots that he never intended to be seen as separate works of art were elevated to that status by the executor. The artist must distinguish what is finished, signed, and completed work versus what is not intended for market.
    —*Stephen E. Weil, Attorney*

Talk to your executor about your priorities. Make sure he or she knows your wishes for your work. You may want to write a letter specifying your intentions and preferences, even though in many states such a letter does not legally bind the executor. If you have named advisors for art-related matters, you can suggest what authority the advisors have and when you would like the executor to follow their advice, although, again, such instructions are not necessarily legally binding.

Left to Right
William Feltzin, Betty Cuningham, David Schaengold, Elizabeth Catlett,
Richard Shebairo, Betty Woodman (back), Harriet Shorr (back)

CHOOSING AN ACCOUNTANT

Estate planning is a process. I think it is a good idea for couples to come in together. It should be a joint effort. At some point, the professionals should be introduced to other family members.
—David Schaengold, C.P.A.

Choose an accountant by giving yourself choices. Ask friends, colleagues, and others for referrals. Make appointments to meet each one—most accountants will not charge for such an interview. <u>Include your spouse in this process.</u>

Find out whether they are competent in income tax planning for artists and estate tax planning. The two plans may need to be integrated, and an accountant with only an income tax focus could hamper your estate planning options.

Look for someone with whom you are comfortable and can relate; someone with the potential for a long-term relationship that can develop beyond income tax planning. Accountants often become a client's closest financial advisor. Use your own judgment through the interview process so that you can make an informed choice.

COSTS TO THE ESTATE

While I feel burdened now with the estates of two of my deceased ancestors, and the imminent estate of a third who is quite elderly, I also have great concerns for my son, who is going to inherit five artists' estates. In dealing with my father's estate, my sister and I were fortunate. The largest problems were storage and insurance. The hope is that the estate can support that expense. You are lucky if it does. And this is before you even begin to think of archiving or inventory, which is expensive to do.
—Hermine Ford, Artist

What do you do with the work of an artist who is not respected, whose production was primarily personal, for whom there is no consensus of opinion of

significance, where there is no money to preserve the work, where there is no group of supporters who want to perpetuate the work? How do you deal with storage? How do you deal with this volume of material?
—Alan Schwartzman, Writer

The reality is, it is almost prohibitively expensive to store art. How do you preserve the work if the money is not there?
—Stephen E. Weil, Attorney

Your estate plan should take into consideration all the costs involved with your estate. In addition to the costs associated with settling any estate—such as funeral expenses, payment of outstanding bills, and estate taxes, if any are due—an artist's estate faces additional costs for the storage, insurance, and appraisal of art works. Your executor, attorney, and accountant are entitled to compensation for their work on your estate, as are any advisors you may select to help with art-related issues.

Often, an estate rich in art works is cash poor. If you anticipate that your estate will not have enough cash to cover the costs of settling your estate, you might consider a simple insurance policy. For example, at age 40, it is possible for a male non-smoker to obtain a $25,000 insurance policy with annual premiums level for fifteen years of $50 every three months. The premium for women is a little less. This kind of insurance can be obtained through many savings and other banks.

If you want to avoid having the proceeds of such an insurance policy subject to tax, it is possible to set up an insurance trust to buy and own the policy. A friend or relative can serve as trustee. You donate enough money for the trustee to buy a policy and make an annual gift to the trust to cover the premium. The trust pays the premium. The policy is not included in your estate because it is owned by the trust. (Ask an accountant or attorney for advice in setting up such a trust.)

Should you feel that your likely taxable estate does not warrant the formation of an insurance trust at this stage, give consideration to a policy payable to your estate (which may ultimately be a bad tax result). But do get a policy if there is no other ready cash source and give consideration to assigning it to an insurance trust as soon as you can.

How is an executor's fee determined?

The executor's fee is usually governed by state law and based on a percentage of the estate's value after specific legacies are distributed. If you leave your art as part of your residual estate (not in a specific legacy), it becomes part of the basis on which your executor will be compensated. In some cases, you may be able to specify the amount of the executor's fee in your will.

How much will storage cost?

The answer to this question depends on the number, size, and material of your works, your financial situation, your location, and your priorities. Ten large-scale sculptures, 100 videos, or 1,000 watercolor paintings require very different storage decisions. No matter what the medium, it is a tremendous help to your executor if you can set aside enough money to store your art for a reasonable period of time; even if you have created a detailed inventory and made plans to distribute the work, it will take time to carry out your instructions. If your work generates reliable income, some of that money can be used to pay for storage. It is important to evaluate your storage needs on a regular basis.

If your work does not generate much income, and you want to make sure it is seen after your death, you can accomplish that goal and reduce storage costs by giving work to institutions, organizations, friends, or family while you are alive. Gifts to children are valued at fair market value, but current tax laws do not allow artists to deduct more than the cost of materials when they donate work to tax-deductible organizations. (See Part II for more information on tax, gift, and valuation issues.)

Left to Right
Erik Stapper, Peter Stevens, Hermine Ford, John Silberman

Do I need to have my work appraised?

Yes. All existing works of art in your estate will have to be appraised, in order to determine the value of your estate for any required estate tax returns. Your executor selects the appraiser. (See Part II, page 72 for more information on valuation and page 75 for information on the appraisal.)

MAINTAINING A REPUTATION

Art is one of the few professions where you can go to the grave with no one interested in your work, but as long as the work exists, there is the opportunity for reassessment. How does an artist keep his or her work visible?
    —Chuck Close, Artist

I am trying very hard to let go of my need to control what happens to my work and my reputation after I die. I hope to be able to turn the backlog into landfill long before that. I have seen the way my own reputation has developed over the last thirty years, and what seems to be true for me personally is that I sell one or two pieces a year and get a great deal more press attention than would be suggested by how much I sell. I have concluded that my main responsibility to the future, so far as I have any, is to make sure there are representations of my work available for art critics, art historians, academics, and needy Ph.D. students. Once I have done that, my job is done.
    —Adrian Piper, Artist

It will work itself out. If the artists take the responsibility to do the best they can to document their career and philosophy, that's all they can do. The individuals or institutions entrusted with this documentation should be chosen based on specific goals, such as: preservation, publication, access for research, exhibition, or other concerns. Knowing what you want helps insure the best outcome.
    —Peter Stevens, Artist

Like everything else in the world, it all has to do with love and money. I have been thinking about setting up some kind of committee to help my children. I don't want them to be burdened with anything to do with this physical body of work. We all need committed, passionate friends to appoint to such a committee. Someone has to love the work, even if there isn't enough money to support the efforts of preserving the work and the artist's reputation—those are the people the artist needs to think about appointing to an advisory group. You can arrange to compensate them with art or money, and set a time limit for them to try to accomplish some of your wishes. And let them know what your wishes are.
—Harriet Shorr, Artist

I am impressed by the contribution the market makes to the preservation of art, which is to endow it with value. To preserve art is expensive. A society can preserve only a small part of its heritage. How do you maintain the value of art when the artist is gone?
Andre Emmerich, Dealer

We have to consider artists who are not in the mainstream, African-American artists and Latin artists. These are people who produce a lot and exhibit. What will happen to their art?
—Elizabeth Catlett, Artist

Most artists below the rank of superstar do not have the money to set up a foundation that would pay warehousing fees and personnel to care for the continuing life and career of the art. Our national, state, and city governments do pay to warehouse their own records, but aside from the selective warehousing (mostly of paper documents) by the Archives of American Art, there is no government warehousing of art from artists' estates. But perhaps with the current possibilities offered by electronic imaging, at least a representative selection of images created by visual artists could be stored and should be started, by a government agency, with provision made to keep these records accessible.
—Philip Pearlstein, Artist

How can I help make sure my work continues to be seen?

If you exhibit and sell your work during your lifetime, your work may continue to be exhibited and sold after your death, if there are people who are willing to manage your artistic estate. If preservation is more important to you than income, it might be possible for your work to be displayed and cared for in local art centers, cultural centers, historical societies, public schools, colleges, universities, or libraries. Hospitals, hospices, residence facilities, and homes for the aged are often receptive to gifts of art as well. If you think your work would be appropriate for a particular location, find out if the organization is interested in having and caring for your work. Art in Perpetuity is an organization that is trying to place the work of unrecognized artists. (See Appendix R for more information, and Appendix S for Resource Directory.)

Can I give my work to a museum?

Some art can be offered as gifts to museums, but the museum has to be willing to accept the art and be able to take care of it; most small museums have storerooms that are not much better than the family's own basement and have no conservation department. And works of art do fall apart.
    —Philip Pearlstein, Artist

One artist was a designer of ceramic plateware. After her death, an international museum wanted her work. We encountered many problems: We had to get out of her loft quickly, since there was no money to pay rent. We gave the work to a single museum, when we should have split it up. I made settlements on royalties I would not have made under other circumstances.
    —David Brown, Attorney

Left to Right
Robert Storr, Emily Mason, Betty Cuningham,

Think of a museum's basement as the library stacks; what is upstairs on display is the equivalent to the reference shelves. In most museums there is a lot of rotation out of the basement to the upstairs or to other museums for special exhibitions. It is better to be in a museum's basement than in a warehouse on Long Island.
 —Robert Storr, Artist and Curator

The focus of most art museums is a particular portion of art history or a type of art-making. Some collect aggressively and broadly, others slowly and more narrowly, and a number of "Institutes" and "Museums" of contemporary art devote themselves primarily, if not exclusively, to exhibiting rather than collecting art. A handful of those that do collect have a policy to de-acquisition their holdings after a certain amount of time has passed, in order to stay contemporary.

It is natural to look to a museum as the possible purchaser of work or the recipient of gifts from your estate, or as the possible host of a posthumous retrospective. However, unnecessary tensions and disappointments can result from approaching the wrong institution altogether, or the right institution at the wrong time. It is important to be thorough in planning any approach to a museum, to be patient but not docile in dealing with them, and to be reasonable in your long-term expectations. And remember, the exhibitions programs, acquisitions budgets, and storage facilities of most museums are limited relative to the number of artists that potentially merit attention.

<u>You may want to avoid making friends, family, or executors negotiate with museums, and the possible damage to your reputation that could result from posthumous rejection by an institution.</u> If so, you should make contact with museums and curators before your death, to make certain that gifts mentioned in a will, or gifts made by heirs according to your instructions, are in fact welcome.

The best first step is to research the full range of museums in your area—city, state, private, university, and college—as well as historical societies, ethnic or socially defined museums, study centers or associations, natural history museums, etc. Next, identify the curators active in those institutions who might be interested in your work. Study their past exhibitions, writings, and involvement in the arts community to find out where their interests lie. Most responsible curators are open to discussing art that is outside their personal taste, but within the scope of their museum, but you want to find a curator who will be an enthusiastic advocate for your work. If you work in more than one medium, it may make sense to talk to curators in each medium.

Remember, in most museums the decision to make a purchase or to accept a gift or to mount an exhibition comes gradually, through internal negotiation and bureaucratic procedure; a quick answer is unlikely, and pressing for one may doom your efforts.

If the answer to your proposal for an acquisition, gift, or exhibition is "No," make sure to ask if other opportunities exist in the more distant future, and if the curator can recommend alternative institutions to approach. Sometimes, the "No" means "not now" rather than "never." Other times, it means "not here" rather than "nowhere." For those who are unfamiliar with the art world and art world manners, it is easy to take offense or draw mistaken conclusions from an initial rejection, but most art professionals will do their best to steer people in more promising directions if they are asked in a forthright way. If the initial answer to your proposal is "Yes," be prepared to be flexible about details.

Gifts. Most museums are reluctant to accept donations of work that has restrictions on where, how, and how often they can display the work. The more restrictions you or your heirs impose, the less likely a museum is to accept even a first-rate work. If you want to negotiate a restriction on whether the institution can de-acquisition the work, remember that a museum may eventually want to sell a donated work in order to acquire a superior one by the artist that appears on the market. Given the costs of installation, conservation, and storage, it is extremely unlikely that a museum would accept a work it did not honestly intend to keep.

Acquisitions. Most museum purchases are decided upon by committees composed of patrons to whom curators present options. Very few museums pay full market value for the works they buy. Thus, museum purchases rarely help establish high prices for the work offered. Partial gifts (with tax benefits) coupled with partial purchase is a standard arrangement, as is the gift of a work or works coupled with the purchase of another work or group of works.

Exhibitions. Any serious presentation of an artist's work takes careful research, time-consuming organization, and, quite frequently, extensive conservation of the work. This means that most curators and museums are already committed to shows several years into the future. Memorial exhibitions closely following an artist's death are the exception rather than the rule, and an agreement to mount a posthumous museum show of whatever size seldom ensures quick, widespread, or lasting public attention for an artist's work. In fact, your reputation may be better served by a "settling" period than by immediate promotional activity. Make sure that those who manage your artistic estate are willing to heed advice about what work to hold back from exposure until a museum show occurs. Be aware that restraint in exercising copyright privileges may be a factor in a museum's decision to mount an exhibition: if the use of images for catalogs, posters, post cards, etc., is overly restricted, it may be difficult for a museum to undertake the project.

In general, it is best for your long-term reputation to place your work in as many appropriate museums and other institutions as possible, whether by purchase or donation. In some cases, however, it may be appropriate for particular bodies of work within your overall production to be concentrated in one place. If you plan to make a tax-deductible donation of your work during your lifetime, remember that you are allowed to deduct only the cost of materials, not the fair market value of the work.

Left to Right
David Brown, John Oddy, Janet Fish, Harriet Shorr

What should I do with my papers?

Any full scholarly or critical understanding of an artist must begin with a complete record of his or her work. Although the basis of that record is an inventory or catalog of the works themselves, your development is also traced through other types of documentation. Accordingly, such documentation should be preserved, not only to maintain your reputation, but to help establish authenticity and expose forgeries.

You should save letters, catalogs, photographs, invitations, diaries and other personal writings, sales records and other related financial transactions, texts of speeches, press clippings, and anything else that will help others understand the historical and social texture of your creative life. These papers can be stored simply in file cabinets or sturdy cardboard boxes. If you have at least fifteen years' worth of papers in your studio, it is likely that you do not need the earlier material anymore, and you should think about offering it to a public library or archive, with the understanding that future deposits will occur in time. If you feel that you cannot part with your papers, you should designate in your will that you want them to be given to a public institution and then name someone to be in charge of this task. This person should be someone whose interest is to make sure that information is protected, not censored, and, ideally, is cognizant of art-historical practices. Potentially embarrassing materials that will hurt the living should not be destroyed; rather, they should be restricted for an appropriate number of years. You should appoint someone you trust to award access to documentary material judiciously, but do not try to over-control the future. If you attach too many conditions or restrictions to your papers, scholars and critics will be unable to use them, and your place in the world as an artist will be perceived incorrectly or incompletely.

The largest and most practical repository for artists' papers is a national one. The Archives of American Art, which is part of the Smithsonian Institution, has branches in Boston, Detroit, Los Angeles, New York City, and Washington, D.C., but it collects materials from artists in all areas of the country. Papers are eventually microfilmed, and the films are

Left to Right
Frank Hodsoll, Bill Jensen, David Brown

available for viewing without charge not only in the branches mentioned above, but throughout the country via interlibrary loan.

Among the other well-known institutions open to receiving artists' papers are the Library of Congress, the New York Public Library, the Beinecke Library (Yale University), Princeton University Library, Boston University, the University of Chicago, the Delaware Art Museum, Syracuse University, the Harry Ransom Humanities Research Center (University of Texas at Austin), and the J. Paul Getty Trust. However, many local museums, libraries, historical societies, and universities are often eager for artists' papers, too. Indeed, you might be able to wrangle a catalog or an exhibition from a library or university in your area in exchange for donating your papers to it. Above all, remember that unless you are a very famous or esteemed artist, if you don't leave your papers to a public library or archive where a curious researcher may find them and decide to publish about you, you hasten your chances of being forgotten.

Lastly, in cases where an artist or an artist's heirs or executors have successfully placed a work with a museum, it is best to give all papers relevant to that particular work—exhibition documentation, reviews, notes on materials used, notes on generative ideas, related correspondence, or copies of such papers—to the museum receiving the work.

TAX ISSUES

I posed this question to the IRS: Suppose you want to try your hand at making small sculptures, although that is not what you are known for and there is a very small market for them. Over many years you make thousands of small sculptures. What happens to them when you die? The response from the IRS was, "If you do not want to pay taxes on them, destroy them before you die."
—John Silberman, Attorney

Everything you own becomes part of your estate. What happens to those things depends on what you decide in writing during your life.
—Frank Hodsoll, County Commissioner;
former chair, National Endowment for the Arts

Current U.S. tax law is burdensome to visual artists on two counts. First, living artists are not allowed to use the fair market value of their work to figure the tax-deductible contribution to a tax-exempt organization, such as a museum or historical society. Living artists are allowed to deduct only the cost of materials. Upon death, however, all their unsold works must be assigned a fair market value for the estate tax return. In some cases, the value assigned to the art can determine whether or not estate taxes are due.

Will my estate have to pay estate taxes?

Federal estate tax returns will have to be filed if your total estate (all property, including art, materials, tools, real estate, insurance proceeds, or other assets) is valued at $600,000 or more (the reporting level gradually increases, beginning in 1998, to reach $1,000,000 in 2006). Whether or not Federal estate tax must be paid on the amount in excess of $600,000 will depend on deductions for debts and expenses, or marital and charitable legacies. There is no Federal estate tax on the transfer of an estate to a surviving spouse who is a U.S. citizen or to a charity regardless of nationality. The surviving spouse also has a $600,000 exemption so that with proper planning, $1,200,000 can be left tax free by a married couple. States vary in the financial requirements for state estate taxes. (See Part II, page 126 for more information on recent changes in the tax laws.)

How will my estate be valued?

The value of your estate is determined by the fair market value of all your assets at the time of your death, including your artwork and any work by other artists that you have acquired during your lifetime. (See Part II, page 72 for more information on valuation.)

How will my works of art be valued?

Whether you sold ten things in your career or thousands, the IRS will be a

factor. The IRS doesn't know what the work is worth as long as you are alive. We try to give it away and they say, "We can't establish a value on this stuff, so you get to take only the cost of the materials that went into the execution of it." When you die, all of a sudden they seem to know exactly what the stuff is worth. They assess your heirs at full market value—not the 50 percent market value that you might be able to get for it, never mind the problems of dumping huge amounts of it on the market at one time. Because I have, on occasion, sold a photograph for an obscenely large amount of money, that doesn't mean that the eight or nine hundred photographs I have in my basement could ever be sold in a hundred lifetimes. Should I just destroy all this work? How can I convince anybody that this work is not major work but may have some kind of historic value?
  —Chuck Close, Artist

The appraisal of art is an inexact and sometimes contested process.
Since your works of art will be appraised at fair market value at the time of your death, you want to make sure that the value given your work in this hypothetical sale is not inflated. If the art has a claimed value of $3,000 or more, an expert appraisal, under oath, must be filed with the estate tax return. In court cases where the IRS has challenged estate appraisals, the court has examined auction records as well as sales by dealers. (See Part II, page 75 for more information.) Your executor will select an appraiser to determine the fair market value of your artwork. Your dealer, if you have one, should act as or work with the appraiser, since the dealer can categorize works as salable or unsalable and help assign a value to each. The appraisal should be reviewed by the lawyer working on the estate as well.

For artists with successful commercial careers or with intermittent careers, there is a danger of an inflated appraisal of unsalable works, based on previous sales. In the 1960s, the concept of "blockage" was introduced in a tax court trial over the estate of artist David Smith. The blockage discount is based on the assumption that if a large number of works by one artist goes on the market at one time, prices for individual works will drop. Alternately, blockage takes into account the possibility of a single buyer purchasing an artist's works for later resale. While the concept of blockage may at times be applied to reduce the value of art, the IRS has occasionally shown a preference to valuation by one-at-a-time retail sales.

If the number and value of your art works comprise a significant portion of your estate, there are various ways you can decrease the potential tax burden incurred by your body of work.

How can I minimize any estate taxes on my artwork?

There was a tax controversy involving Jacquelyn Susann, who instructed her executor to destroy her diaries. The executor did, but the IRS still assessed a value on them, quite a high one. The IRS prevailed because the diaries existed at the time of her death.
    —David Schaengold, C.P.A.

We started off concerned about our son, Charlie, for three reasons: first, that the taxes on the art would consume much or all of the liquid assets that he might inherit. Second, that he might be pressured into hasty and unreflective sales to meet that tax obligation. Third, that he might not be able to effectively manage three estates. Our solution has two parts: one, a nonprofit charitable foundation; and two, wills that are quite specific about how art may be given to the foundation. In general terms, our son and heir may choose up to a certain percentage of the three artistic estates. The remaining parts will be given to the foundation. The foundation, combined with wills, ensures that a specific portion of our artistic estate will be treated as a cultural issue and not a financial matter. The foundation must give away what income it realizes.
    —Betty Woodman, Artist

We started a foundation with $60,000. We give small grants annually, but we can leverage certain ideas. It doesn't take a lot of money to encourage people to write critical articles that benefit the field.
    —Kate Horsfield, Artist

If a board of directors is set up, it should be a widely dispersed board of directors, not just people who are intimately involved, because emotions get tangled up in issues of control. It is not about the work, it is about control.
    —Bill Jensen, Artist

I decided to set up a revocable trust and asked some people if they would be willing to be trustees. I tried to pick people who were younger than I am.
    —Janet Fish, Artist

The clarity of purpose of a foundation is essential. It is important to pick an executor and subsequently trustees who will carry out that mission and be steadfast.
    —Charles Bergman, The Pollock-Krasner Foundation

For married artists who wish for their estate to go to their surviving spouse, estate taxes will not be an immediate problem, since there is no estate tax on property passing to a surviving spouse who is a U.S. citizen. For others (unmarried artists, artists in gay or lesbian partnerships, or artists with a surviving spouse who is an alien or does not want the responsibility of caring for the work), this is not an option. There are other ways to reduce estate taxes by removing art from your estate. The following descriptions do not constitute an exhaustive list of tax-planning measures; they are offered as examples. (See Part II, page 61 for more information on strategies to minimize estate taxes.)

   Gifts. You can make gifts of your work to institutions, your children, or other people. Under current tax law you can take a charitable deduction on your income taxes for a gift to a nonprofit organization, but only for the amount of the materials used to create the work; you cannot deduct the fair market value of the work. You can make a gift of art pieces having a fair market value of up to $10,000 a year per

Left to Right
Nancy Fried, Avis Berman, Kate Horsfield, Joan Jonas, Cynthia Carlson, Janet Fish,
Emily Mason (back), Allan Schwartzman (back)

person ($20,000 if the gift is from you and your spouse), to as many people as you wish, without incurring the Federal gift tax (after 1998 the annual amount is indexed for inflation). In addition, if a work is valued at $30,000, you can make the gift over a three-year period, at $10,000 each year. You will need to document the transfer of the work and its valuation.

The status of the artwork, which is received as a gift from the artist, is treated as "ordinary income property" for the person who receives the gift. However, if that person gives the property to a museum, the value of the donation is still the value of the materials.

Creating a Trust. A trust divides the management of assets and the benefit derived from those assets. For example, to be entitled to a marital deduction for transfers to an alien spouse, a trust must be used to guarantee payment of the U.S. estate tax on the death of the survivor. Also, if you want to leave your estate to children who are not capable of or not interested in managing your artistic legacy, a trust can direct income to those beneficiaries, with trustees managing the assets. It is important to remember that control of the art will rest with the trustees. Putting art into a trust can reduce estate taxes, but the trust will provide income to the beneficiaries only if the art is able to generate income through, for example, sales or reproductions. (The trust set up to hold a simple term life insurance policy to provide money for storage, described in Costs to the Estate, similarly removes an asset—an insurance policy—from your estate.)

Trusts can have either charitable or noncharitable purposes, and consequently may or may not qualify for tax-exempt status. Noncharitable trusts, as contrasted to charitable trusts, must pay income tax on income from the sale of art, and can distribute income to noncharitable beneficiaries.

Creating a Foundation. A foundation is a nonprofit corporation or trust governed by a board of trustees which may qualify for Federal tax-exempt status and may qualify to receive tax-deductible donations. Though lawyers often discourage the creation of a foundation with under one million dollars in assets, the amount of money needed to set up a foundation depends on what you want the foundation to do. The value and income-generating potential of the assets held by a foundation will determine the number and size of the grants it can award. A foundation can be set up fairly easily, and may be in a better position to ensure the continued preservation and exhibition of your work than individual beneficiaries. As with a non-charitable trust, the control and management of the assets is in the hands of the trustees.

Assets transferred by a will to a nonprofit foundation are exempt from estate taxes and from income taxes when sold. Such foundations are chartered to benefit the public good and must have a charitable purpose. No foundation's profit may benefit individuals, and they are not a tax shelter for personal business. They are subject to the supervision of the attorneys general of the various states, but not all have an active staff similar to the Charities Bureau of the New York Attorney General. If you want to contribute to the continuation of certain ideas or activities, which benefit the public instead of specific beneficiaries, you can set up a nonprofit foundation. (See Part II, page 87 for more information.)

IN A MORE PERFECT WORLD: CHANGING PUBLIC POLICY

Current tax law in the United States works against the preservation of the cultural heritage of this country. A successful living artist is allowed to deduct only the cost of materials when donating art to a nonprofit organization such as a museum, school, or community center, denying the artist any tax benefit for the preservation of the work in the public interest. For artists whose work has not found a market, however, the problem is that the work is likely to be dispersed, lost, or destroyed. "They die, and the stuff sits in a garage or basement until it rots away. There has to be some way to do better than that, some kind of documentation. Even a disk of images preserved somewhere would be something," commented artist **Philip Pearlstein**. A disk of information could at least facilitate historic and aesthetic research.

Betty Cuningham, associate director of the Hirschl & Adler Modern, liked the idea of a national archive that would allow access to artists' materials, permitting art historians to reevaluate an artist's career. Other imagined strategies for the preservation of the visual art production of this country included a suggestion by Beverly Wolff, Esq., general counsel of The Museum of Modern Art, for a short-term depository, offering storage for the time needed to dispose of an artist's estate. Communities across the country could be linked to a system of archives through the library system, asserted artist Joan Jonas. Colleges and universities could be responsible for archiving the work of their own art faculty. According to Charles Bergman, executive vice president of The Pollock-Krasner Foundation, it might be possible to establish a network of community foundations for the preservation of work. Fred Lazarus, president of the Maryland Institute College of Art, speculated about the possibility of an institutional trusteeship or a nonprofit agency that would function much as a bank serves as an estate trustee, but with specialized knowledge about managing artists' estates. Such an entity could be designated to provide such services as inventory, storage, or promotion for a foundation or for individual heirs on a fee basis. The Estate Project for Artists with AIDS is in its second year of giving grants to institutions and organizations to test various methods of dealing with artists' estates, reported coordinator Cesar Trasobares. For example, the New York Public Library received a grant to rescue entire archives, including artists' work, journals, notes, and books. Grants have also been given to the New York Library for the Performing Arts, Dance Notation Bureau, and Volunteer Lawyers for the Arts. Irving Sandler summarized the conversation by saying that in the interest of preserving the sketches, studies, trial proofs, installation bits, and unsuccessful or incompletely realized works of art for future art historical study, a tax category should be established for such works designated by the artist(s) or their heirs to be outside the commercial realm and therefore, untaxable. (Such laws do exist in Europe.)

In debating the likelihood of changing present tax law, which restricts an artist's charitable donation of work to the cost of the materials, to instead allow a charitable deduction of the fair market value of the work, artists **Harriet Shorr** and **Chuck Close**, and **Barbara Hoffman**, Esq., all suggested framing the debate in terms of public policy, rather than finances. "American institutions are being deprived of works of art because it is not financially desirable for artists to give gifts," **Hoffman** pointed out. Commissioner of Ouray County, Colorado, and former National Endowment for the Arts chairman **Frank Hodsoll** explained that the IRS argument is that fair market value is calculated as the cost of the materials plus the value added by the artist's manipulation of the materials. When an artist donates an object to a museum, he or she has not paid income tax on the added value, and consequently should not be able to deduct that value. He does not believe the IRS would ever allow artists to deduct the fair market value of their donated work for income tax purposes. **Robert Storr**, artist and curator at The Museum of Modern Art, argued that "if the issue is presented solely in terms of possible economic benefit to the individual, you will spend forever in a maze of legalism." Rather, he maintained, the argument should focus on the fact that the United States is losing irreplaceable parts of its cultural heritage by making it difficult for artists to donate works to American museums. While some critics of tax policy see the benefits of museum donations favoring affluent collectors—and, potentially, affluent artists, should the law be changed and fair market value-based deductions be extended to them—the biggest loser is the general public, present and future, whose access to the masterworks produced in their own country is being forever compromised by short-term, and comparatively small budgetary advantages to the Treasury. **Lazarus** suggested convening an artist committee and a museum committee to work on this issue.

Another proposal was that the IRS should accept art as payment for estate taxes. Artist **Elizabeth Catlett** noted that the Mexican government accepts art in payment for taxes. The IRS could then give the work to museums or libraries, agreed artist **Bill Jensen**. "Whenever you make a change in the tax law that saves tax," warned **Erik Stapper** (Stapper & Van Doren), "you have to make up for it in some other place. Revenue loss has to be offset by revenue gain." But **Richard Shebairo**, C.P.A., P.C., encouraged artists "to unite to make their voices heard," and believes that getting the IRS to accept art as payment for estates taxes is an idea worth pursuing. Noting that gay and lesbian artists are denied the marital exemption of $1.2 million on their estates, **Hodsoll** suggested investigating other ways to achieve a deduction, perhaps through a partnership structure.

The problem with taxes, said **Trasobares,** is indicative of a larger prob- lem: how art and artists are viewed in American society. "I think you have to consider artists who are not in the mainstream. African-American and Latin artists. What will happen to their art? They have never been fully recognized as part of the U.S. art world," observed **Catlett**. Artist **Adrian Piper** felt artists should be "realistic about how much public policy can help. It has to be thought of as the individual artist's problem." **Storr,** while granting that "short-term solutions will fall on individuals," believes that there is long-term hope for changing policy. **Jonas,** too, commented that education at the grass roots can change policy; the problem, she said, is that artists have not been organized in making their arguments.

David Schaengold, C.P.A. (David Tarlow & Co. P.C.), explained that the estate tax is not legally defined as a tax on property or inheritance, but on the privilege of an individual to transfer his or her estate. Should an artist's body of work be defined as personal property or as an interest in a business? An estate transferring a business interest is allowed to pay the estate tax in installments over a fifteen-year period. Schaengold argued that an artist is in the business of creating art, and his or her art works should be valued as an interest in a business, not as personal property—that is, the art works are created for the production of income in the course of the artist's occupation. "When an artist dies, the interest in the business should be valued," he said. "If that were the case, the tax would be much lower because the value would be based on what the artist was earning during his or her lifetime—historical earnings, not future earnings." Currently, works of art in an artist's estate are valued no differently than works of art in a collector's estate; both are valued as personal property.

Many participants were intrigued with Schaengold's suggestion, although several added that such an approach would probably require litigation. Nonetheless, Schaengold stressed that "this requires no change in law—an artist is already treated as being in business for income tax purposes. Wouldn't the courts want to treat artists the same way when they die as they were treated while they were alive?" **Hoffman** was supportive of the idea, but cautioned about the need for consistency in interpretation and advocacy. For example, what effect does taking the artist in a business position for estate tax purposes have on other provisions of the tax code as applied to artists?

Hodsoll pointed out that it might be more cost-effective to lobby for legislation to clarify an artist's position as having an interest in a business. In the area of estate tax reform, artists' chances for success would be improved by joining with others involved in similar efforts, such as the National Federation of Independent Business and the Farm Bureau, and by marshaling the support of arts service, funding, and lobbying organizations, including the National Association of Artists' Organizations, Grantmakers in the Arts, and Americans for the Arts.

A Visual Artist's Guide to Estate Planning

Part II

INTRODUCTION TO PART II
"Ars longa, vita brevis"

In the past twenty years, art law has emerged as a distinct area of the law covering works of fine art and those who create, purchase and sell them. The contours of the law are difficult to define, since art law always begins with the application of some other type of law—copyright law, tax law and estate and trust law—to the artist. For this reason, the collaboration of the Committee on Art Law of the Association of the Bar of the City of New York and The Marie Walsh Sharpe Art Foundation on this book is particularly beneficial.

Visual art clients, like any other clients, do not want to think about dying. Yet, for the visual artist whose entire career has been devoted to his or her art and its integrity without thought of commercial success and, even more often, without the financial rewards which accompany such success, dying without a will or other legal arrangement executed by the artist during his or her life, can result in the most personal of future decisions being made by the state. For individuals with modest wealth and uncomplicated business relationships, this standard estate plan"[1] may be satisfactory, but for most others, particularly the visual artist whose principal estate asset may be art created by him or her, the "standard estate plan" is unsatisfactory.

To write a formally valid simple form will is not difficult; however, when you go to a lawyer to plan your estate and to write your will, you are really setting in motion a much more complex process. Estate planning is the application of the attorney's expertise to the artist client's informed objectives. Generally there is more than one way to meet a client's objectives. The challenge is to recharacterize the estate planning process from one which is preoccupied with dying to one which empowers the visual artist to take steps now that can impact future public recognition of the artist and the appreciation of the artist's work.

---

[1] See J. H. Merryman and A. Elsen, Law, *Ethics and the Visual Arts,* Vol. 2, p. 445 (1987).

Thus, estate planning for the visual artist often requires special considerations in addition to providing for family and friends and avoiding unnecessary tax, probate, and administration expenses. These concerns derive
from the way the visual artist earns income and the nature of the assets
included in the artist's estate: The choice of executors; creation and operation of artist foundations; preserving and placing the artist's work; management of copyright and other intellectual property; sufficient liquidity
to pay debts and administration expenses; valuation of the estate for
estate tax purposes, are some of the special concerns of visual artists
expressed in Part I.

Various strategies are available to the artist to address these concerns.
One estate planning technique available to the artist is to make gifts of
works during his or her lifetime. Such a gift will preclude further appreciation in the work from being included in the artist's gross estate, and if
the gift falls within certain statutory limitations, it may not be subject to
taxation at all. The artist may also be able to set up a family partnership
or foundation. Finally, if the artist has the ability to forego profits from
the sale of the artist's works during his or her lifetime, the artist's estate
or beneficiaries can sell the property at potentially significant tax savings
after his or her death. Carefully planning for disposition and preservation
of the artwork and exploitation of the artist's intellectual property can
produce income for the estate and beneficiaries or sustain a private foundation created to promote the artist's work and ideas.

In Part II we provide a more in-depth legal analysis of these techniques
and an overview of strategies relating to estate planning and the administration of the artist's estate. Many of the legal issues are intricate and
complex and an exhaustive legal review and analysis is beyond the scope
of this book. Part II addresses estate planning and administration for the
visual artist with a discussion of six broad topics: (i) Overview of Tax and
Estate Planning (Baltz and Fraiman), (ii) Checklist for Artists' Gifts of
Artwork (Wolff), (iii) Valuation (Baltz) and Appraisal (Wolf), (iv) Artists'
Foundations (Baltz, Bjorklund), (v) Copyright and Other Intellectual
Property Issues (Hoffman), and (vi) Conflict of Interest (Stapper).
Following this, is a discussion of the 1997 Federal and New York State tax

law changes as they affect the visual artist (Stapper). A glossary is included to assist the artist in understanding terms with which he or she may be unfamiliar. Additional forms, including a power of attorney, health care proxy, copyright, and other resource materials are provided.

We have tried in the discussion of the selected topics and the comments which follow them to show that there is no single right strategy to meet the artist client's objectives: the importance placed by individual artists on the concerns set forth above varies, as does the size of the estate and the family situation. Moreover, the complexity of the income, gift and estate tax laws, combined with the intricacies of copyright law and artistic and intellectual property management offer the possibility of multiple solutions.[2]

For example, perhaps the most critical decision in estate planning for the artist is the choice of an executor, trustee, and successor executors and trustees or director of the artist's foundation. These individuals or institutions will be charged with all critical decisions which affect the artist's work, and thus, ultimately, the artistic merit and legacy of the artist. Whether to select family, friends, or professional advisors, or an institution as executor or trustee or to select co-executors or multiple trustees or directors is based on the artist's situation and needs. Each of the fiduciaries selected owes a duty of undivided loyalty to the estate and the beneficiary; yet, for a trusted advisor or art dealer, apparent conflict of interest (not the prohibition against actual self-dealing) can be waived. There is no one correct choice; however, the wrong choice may harm the artist's work and reputation and lead to costly legal battles.

Anecdotal information (The Dorothy Dehner Foundation) following the topic of Artists' Foundations has been included to illustrate that despite the conventional wisdom that only relatively wealthy artists with assets in excess of two million dollars can contemplate a foundation, it is possible to create a private foundation, a private operating foundation or a charity where "sweat equity" combined with careful management of artistic and

---

[2] In writing this book, examples and forms are based on the New York law of trusts and estates; nevertheless, the issues, if not the identical solutions, should be similar in other states of the United States.

intellectual property assets may compensate, in part, for an absence of cash. Foundations may meet a variety of personal and financial objectives of artists under certain circumstances and the cost and ease of creating and maintaining such foundations has been simplified, despite the contrary impression created by the legal disputes and attendant publicity involved in the Estates of Rothko, Warhol, Cornell, and Mapplethorpe.

The information contained in this book is not a substitute for competent legal advice. Because we have deliberately kept our discussion simple, areas which are extraordinarily complex may appear deceptively easier to understand than they actually are. We recommend that every artist consult with an attorney with regard to his or her estate plan and provide the checklists and clauses following each chapter as a basis for engaging the dialogue.[3] We hope that Part II will encourage and make it easier for all artists to deal with the questions that are presented, regardless of the size of their estates and their art form, although the target audience for this publication is primarily the visual artist—emerging or mid-career. We hope that this book is also useful to attorneys working with artists by making them more aware of artists' specific concerns and providing them with the basic information to address those concerns.

I should personally like to thank the members of the Committee on Art Law who contributed as authors to this book and acted as the Publication Review Committee, and the other members of the Committee and Association who contributed to and commented on it. Above all, I would like to thank the Artist Advisory Committee of The Marie Walsh Sharpe Art Foundation, The Judith Rothschild Foundation and Joyce E. Robinson, without whom this book might have remained an inchoate idea.

Barbara Hoffman,
Chair, Committee on Art Law
Association of the Bar of the City of New York

---

[3] Caveat. Tax laws change. The information provided here is current for May, 1998. Income, gift and estate tax considerations change over time. For example, several years ago, the artist corporation was a technique adapted for both income and estate tax considerations. Today changes in the tax laws, as well as tax court rulings discourage this strategy except in those cases where the artist seeks to obtain the protection from personal liability offered by the corporate form of organization.

OVERVIEW OF TAX AND ESTATE PLANNING
Christina M. Baltz, Esq., and Genevieve L. Fraiman, Esq.

Testamentary and Other Transfers Taking Effect at Death

An artist should make a last will if he or she wishes to determine who will be entitled to the assets of his or her estate, whether outright or in trust, and who as executor and/or trustee will control its administration.

In the absence of a will, under New York's statutory scheme[4], an artist's assets will be distributed on death to the following "distributees": (a) the first $50,000 and one-half of the residue to the spouse, and one-half of the residue to the issue by representation; (b) if there are no issue, the whole to the spouse; (c) if there is no spouse, the whole to the issue by representation; (d) if there are neither spouse nor issue, to the parent or parents; (e) in the absence of spouse, issue, and parents, one-half to the maternal grandparents or if neither survives to their children and grand-children by representation, and one-half to paternal grandparents or if neither survives to their children and grandchildren by representation; and (f) if the nearest relatives are great-grandchildren, one-half to the maternal great-grandchildren per capita and one-half to the paternal great-grandchildren per capita. In categories (e) and (f), if there are no relatives on one side, the whole will pass to the relatives on the other side. Adopted persons, relatives of the half blood and certain non-marital children are treated as if they were relatives of the whole blood.

In an intestate administration (where there is no will), the Surrogate will grant letters of administration to one or more relatives in the following order: (a) the surviving spouse; (b) children; (c) grandchildren; (d) father or mother; (e) brothers or sisters; (f) distributees who are issue of grand-parents. When letters are not granted under these provisions, the public administrator of the county is usually appointed to administer the estate.[5]

---

4 Sections 4-1.1 and 4-1.2 of the New York Estates, Powers and Trusts Law

5 Section 1001 of the New York Surrogate's Court Procedure Act

By avoiding intestacy, a will enables the artist to determine exactly who will receive the estate assets, and under what terms and conditions. Will the spouse receive the entire estate, to the exclusion of the children? Will the children's share be held in trust, and subject to the discretion of the trustee? Will one child be excluded or receive less than his or her siblings? Friends or charities can receive gifts under the will, outright or in trust, to the exclusion of the distributees, other than a surviving spouse who has a statutory right to elect against the will and take his or her elective share.[6] The will could make gifts of specific works of art, a house, a cooperative apartment or condominium, or specified amounts of cash or shares of the estate property to designated individuals or charities. The artist could create a foundation or a charitable remainder trust. The will can determine how estate and other death taxes will be paid. The will can structure the estate in such a way as to promote the artist's works of art.

A will allows the artist to appoint the individuals who, or the bank or trust company which, as executor and/or trustee, will administer the estate and carry out the terms of the will. Selection of an executor, in whose honesty, integrity and judgment, the artist has confidence, is of the utmost importance. If the artist believes that the dealer who has promoted his (or her) art or a fellow artist is best qualified to administer the estate despite a possible conflict of interest, the will could excuse such conflict. The will can grant the fiduciaries broad powers of administration, or can limit the powers of a fiduciary given specific authority only with respect to works of art and copyright matters.

The importance of having a will has been emphasized—and rightfully so since generally the will principally controls the disposition of a person's assets at his or her death—however, not all assets pass by the terms of a person's will. For example, unless an insurance policy names the insured person's estate as the beneficiary of the policy, the proceeds of the policy

---

[6] Section 5-1.1A of the New York Estates, Powers and Trusts Law.

will pass at the insured person's death to the person(s) designated as beneficiary of the policy. The same is true of pensions, IRAs and Keogh plans, which also pass pursuant to beneficiary designations, rather than by the terms of a person's will. A person's interest in certain property (such as real property or bank accounts) that is held jointly with another person as "joint tenants with right of survivorship" or as "tenants by the entirety" will pass at one tenant's death to the other tenant; the deceased tenant's will has no effect on this property.

Lifetime Transfers

Lifetime gifts (charitable and non-charitable) can be an important part of managing and disposing of an artist's assets. Art (or other assets) gifted by an artist during life will not be subject to estate tax at the artist's death.

Outright gifts to family members and friends. There is an unlimited marital deduction for outright gifts to a U.S. citizen spouse or gifts in certain prescribed forms (e.g., a trust for a U.S. citizen spouse who is given a general power of appointment, a joint tenancy or tenancy by the entireties, a QTIP trust, a joint and survivor annuity, or a charitable remainder trust if the spouse is the only non-charitable beneficiary). While there is no marital deduction for gifts to a non-U.S. citizen spouse, annual exclusion gifts of $100,000 may be made to the non-citizen spouse. Gifts to persons other than the donor's spouse are potentially subject to gift tax. However, a person may give a gift of up to $10,000 (or property, including the artist's own artwork with a fair market value of up to $10,000) or, in the case of a married couple, $20,000, to any number of people free of gift tax.[7] These gifts are often referred to as "annual exclusion gifts" since the $10,000/$20,000 gifted is the amount (per donee) which may be excluded each year in determining a person's gifts subject to gift tax.[8] The annual exclusion may only be used during a person's life; there is no comparable

---

[7] If the fair market value of the work is greater than $10,000, the artist can give a fractional interest in the work each year.

[8] Beginning in 1997, the annual exclusion amount was indexed for inflation. It will increase in increments of $1,000 every two to four years (approximately) if the inflation rate remains at relatively low levels.

exclusion from estate taxes for gifts made at a person's death. In addition to the annual gift tax exclusion, the unified credit against Federal estate and gift taxes (discussed below under "Taxes") allows each person to gift $625,000 (gradually increasing to $1,000,000 in 2006) free of Federal gift tax. (If the unified credit is not used to make lifetime gifts, it will be applied against Federal estate taxes.)

For income tax purposes, the donee of a gift retains the donor's basis: i.e., the cost of the materials. In the case of an inheritance, an heir's cost basis will be the fair market value for estate tax purposes. An exchange of artwork between two artists will be treated as a sale, so that both realize taxable ordinary income.

Outright gifts to charitable organizations. Under current law an artist gets an income tax charitable deduction for a gift of his or her art to a charitable organization equal only to his or her cost basis (i.e., the cost of the materials) in the art.[9] (A collector, by contrast, is entitled to an income tax charitable equal to the fair market value of the art at the time of the gift, assuming the gifted art will be put to a use by the donee organization that is related to its charitable purpose.) If an artist receives as a gift work from another artist, credited by that artist, the

---

[9] Editor's comment. Prior to 1969, an artist was allowed to deduct the fair market value of a gift of his or her art to a museum. Several bills have been proposed in Congress to alter the effects of the 1969 changes to the income tax laws; none has been able to garner the support necessary for passage. The proposals have ranged from restoring the artist to the position she held before the passage of the Act, that is to be treated in the same way as a collector, or to providing a credit against the donating artist's income tax. Even though every proposal contained provisions to eliminate abuses, each has died in committee. The most recent bill was introduced in July of 1985, and proposed income tax changes which would provide living artists with a fair market value charitable contribution deduction for the donation of their works to cultural institutions. Specific stipulations had been included to prevent deductions for quickly produced works of art. The donated item had to be directly related to the primary purpose of the accepting institution, and no deduction might be taken by an official of the Federal government if the work was produced during his term in office. The language of the Act states that "[s]ubsection (e) of section 170 of the Internal Revenue Code of 1954 . . . is amended by adding . . . that in the case of a qualified artistic charitable contribution . . . the amount of such contribution shall be the fair market value of the property contributed." H.R. 3087, 99th Cong., 1st Sess. @ 2 (1985).

recipient will have a cost basis in the acquired work equal to the other artist's cost basis in the work and, if the recipient makes a charitable gift of the other artist's work, his or her income tax charitable deduction will be limited to that tax cost basis, rather than the fair market value of the artwork. Although a charitable income tax deduction limited to cost basis does not offer much of an income tax savings incentive for making a gift of art, there are of course other reasons for an artist to make a gift of his or her art, such as benefitting the charitable donee and building a relationship with a charitable donee that benefits the artist's reputation through exhibition of the work and/or that creates a possible repository for the artist's work after death.

Gifts in trust for family members or friends. A gift of art may be made to an irrevocable trust established by the artist for the benefit of family members or other loved ones. A gift made to such a trust in excess of the annual exclusion and unified credit amounts discussed above will be subject to gift tax, but the gifted property will be removed from the artist's estate and therefore will not be subject to estate taxes at the artist's death. From a gift/estate tax standpoint, it is advantageous to make such a gift before an artist's reputation is established and his or her art has not yet achieved a high market value. The art would be held, maintained, and managed by the trustee(s) and eventually (preferably after the art has appreciated) sold or distributed to the beneficiaries. Money or other liquid assets would also need to be gifted to the trust to cover the trust's administrative costs and the costs of maintaining the art before disposition.

Gifts to "split-interest" trusts benefitting both charity and family members or friends. Split-interest trusts may either be "charitable lead trusts" or "charitable remainder trusts". In the case of a charitable lead trust, one or more charitable beneficiaries gets a "lead" interest in the trust (which must be in the form of an annual payment from the trust equal to a fixed percentage of the value of the property in the trust, valued upon contribution to the trust in the case of an "annuity" trust or valued annually in the case of a "unitrust") for a term of years and, after that term of years, the donor's loved ones, as the remainder beneficiaries, get the remaining trust assets. In the case of a charitable remainder trust, the donor and/or his or her loved ones get the lead annuity or unitrust interest in the trust for a term of years (not to exceed twenty years) or for life and, at the end of the term, the charitable beneficiary or beneficiaries get the remaining trust assets. Split-interest trusts afford gift tax and income tax savings where highly appreciating assets (and, in the case of charitable lead trusts, generally income-producing assets) are transferred to the trust. If an artist's work is not marketable and likely to appreciate significantly, a split-interest trust funded with art is not a good disposition of the art. In addition, the charitable income tax deduction advantages to these structures are not available to artists who contribute their own artwork to a split-interest trust because the income tax deduction is limited to the artist's cost basis (as described above).

Revocable trusts for the artist's lifetime benefit and ultimate benefit of others: a will substitute. An artist can contribute his or her art (and other assets) to a revocable trust of which the artist is the beneficiary during his or her lifetime. The artist will generally be the trustee of the trust until his or her death (or incapacity if the artist should become incompetent). Since the trust is initially solely for the artist's own benefit, there is no gift tax due upon the transfer of assets to the trust. As a revocable trust, the terms of the trust may be amended and/or the trust may be revoked by the artist at any time. During the artist's lifetime, the revocable trust allows for centralized management of the artist's artwork (and other assets) and also a plan of management and disposition of the trust assets in the event that the artist becomes incompetent (at which point the second or successor trustee would take control and carry out the terms of the trust). After the artist dies, the revocable trust essentially functions as a will substitute—the trustee disposes of the artist's assets (held in the trust) in accordance with the terms of the trust, and dispositions of trust assets other than to the artist's spouse or charity are subject to estate tax. Although a revocable trust functions as a will substitute, an artist who establishes a revocable trust should nevertheless still have a will that bequeaths any property held by the artist at his or her death to the trustee(s) of the revocable trust. Inevitably there will be some property that did not get transferred to the revocable trust and, without a will, that property will be disposed of under the laws of intestacy, rather than in accordance with the artist's wishes.

Other Estate Planning-Related Documents

Although they are not the subject of this publication, there are certain other estate planning-related documents that an artist should consider executing when executing his or her will or revocable trust. By executing a power of attorney, an artist can appoint one or more persons to act as his or her attorney(s)-in-fact to manage the artist's business and personal financial affairs in the event of the artist's incapacity. (If desired, an attorney-in-fact can also act for a person while the person is competent.) By executing a health care proxy, an artist can appoint one or more persons to act as his or her health care agent to make medical and health care decisions on the artist's behalf in the event of the artist's incapacity. If desired, an artist may also execute a "living will" by which the artist expresses his or her wishes concerning life support and other medical issues. The living will can be helpful in guiding the artist's health care agent. The formal and substantive requirements of powers of attorney, health care proxies, and living wills are governed by state law and therefore vary to some degree from to state to state.

Administration of the Artist's Estate

Administering an estate involves carrying out the terms of the will—that is, wrapping up the artist's financial affairs and managing and disposing of the artist's assets. In basic terms, the executor gathers the artist's assets; pays the artist's debts and estate administration expenses from estate assets; has the artist's assets appraised; pays out the legacies (gifts) to the beneficiaries named in the artist's will; prepares and files Federal and state estate tax returns and (if due) pays Federal and state estate taxes from estate assets; prepares and files the artist's final Federal and state income tax returns and the estate's Federal and state income tax returns and pays any income taxes due from estate assets; distributes the balance of the estate assets to the "residuary" beneficiary of the estate; and prepares an accounting of his or her activities as executor which the residuary beneficiary reviews; and, once the accounting is approved (which absolves the executor from any liability for his or her activities as executor), closes the estate. An executor's checklist of activities follows this discussion.

Taxes[10]

Federal and state (if applicable) estate taxes are calculated as a percentage of the value of an artist's taxable estate. An artist's taxable estate is the fair market value of all property interests he holds at his date of death, less (i) certain estate administration expenses, indebtedness and taxes paid by his estate; and (ii) the value of bequests made to the artist's surviving U.S. citizen spouse; and (iii) the value of bequests made to charitable organizations. The marital deduction for a U.S. citizen spouse is unlimited if the transfer to the spouse under the will or by intestacy is outright or in a prescribed form identical to those allowed for the gift tax marital deduction (e.g., a trust for the spouse who is given a general power of appointment, life insurance or annuity payments with general power of appointment, a QTIP trust, or a charitable remainder trust if the spouse is the only beneficiary other than the charity. There is also an unlimited marital deduction for property passing to a non U.S. citizen spouse provided the property is held in the form of a QDOT that is subjected to estate tax on principal distributions and on the death of the spouse at the marginal estate tax rates of the first deceased spouse.

An artist's estate will be subject to Federal estate taxes if the artist has utilized his unified credit against estate and gift taxes to make lifetime gifts or, if the unified credit has not been used, if the value of the artist's taxable estate exceeds $625,000 (gradually increasing to reach $1,000,000 in 2006). Under current law, the estate of an artist domiciled

---

[10] This discussion applies to estates of artists who at the time of death are U.S. citizens or residents and whose spouses (if any) are U.S. citizens or residents. Different rules apply in the case of nonresident aliens or if a surviving spouse is not a U.S. citizen.

in New York will also be subject to New York estate taxes if the value of his New York taxable estate exceeds $115,000.[11] Effective October 1, 1998, the New York estate tax will be imposed on taxable estates exceeding $300,000, and effective February 1, 2000, an estate will pay no New York estate tax in addition to the Federal tax it pays (New York State will instead receive a portion of the estate taxes otherwise paid to the Internal Revenue Service).

Federal and New York estate taxes are imposed at graduated rates, depending on the value of the taxable estate. The Federal rates range from 18% (imposed on the first $10,000) to 55% (imposed on taxable estates in excess of $3,000,000). New York estate tax rates—in effect until February 1, 2000—range from 2% (imposed on the first $50,000) to 21% (imposed on taxable estates in excess of $10,100,000).

The Federal estate tax return must be filed within nine months of the artist's date of death, unless an extension is granted, and estate taxes generally must be paid at that time. A deposit on the New York estate tax is due within six months of the artist's date of death and the balance is due with the filed return within nine months of the date of death unless an extension is granted.[12]

Thus, valuation of an artist's assets is determinative of the estate taxes payable on the artist's estate (if taxable). If the artist's estate is taxable, there will need to be sufficient liquidity (i.e., cash or marketable assets) to raise the cash necessary to pay estate taxes within nine months of the artist's death.

---

[11] For purposes of determining the New York taxable estate, a deduction of up to $250,000 is allowed for a principal residence that is left to someone other than a spouse or a charitable organization. A nonresident artist who has work in an exhibition or stored in New York State at the time of death may also be subject to New York State estate tax on those works of art.

[12] However, if the value of an artist's artwork exceeds 35% of his adjusted gross estate (i.e., his gross estate less deductions for estate administration expenses, debts and certain taxes) and his artistic enterprise can qualify as a closely held business for purposes of the Internal Revenue Code provision allowing for installment payments of estate taxes, then his estate can defer payment of estate taxes (but not interest) for up to five years and can pay estate taxes in up to ten annual installments, with interest imposed at reduced rates.

COMMENTARY ON TAX AND ESTATE PLANNING[13]
The Artist's Spouse/Partner
Gil Edelson, Esq.

In many cases, the artist's spouse or significant other will be the principal or sole heir. In the case of a spouse, this makes sense both from the personal and the estate tax point of view, since there is no estate tax payable on works left to the spouse.

It is also not uncommon for the spouse or partner to be named as the executor. This is useful because the spouse/partner will probably want to waive an executor's fee. Executors' fees are calculated as a percentage of the total value of the estate; a waiver of the fee saves money, in some cases a substantial sum.

It should be kept in mind that the artist's spouse/partner frequently controls the eventual disposition of the work in the estate. Whether or not the spouse/partner is the beneficiary, he or she will obviously have much to say about what happens to the estate. For example, if the spouse/partner is the executor, he or she will select the lawyer for the estate. He or she is also likely to select the dealer through whom work will be sold. The spouse/partner will have the artist's records and may be asked for information or provenance. The spouse/partner could be asked to authenticate or to assist in authentication. He or she may also be critical in supplying information for scholarly publications, articles, and a *catalogue raisonné*. The spouse or partner will also control the copyrights in the artist's works.

For the foregoing reasons, the artist may wish to leave detailed instructions to his or her spouse/partner, although they are not binding.

In addition, it is important for the spouse or partner to plan his or her estate since that estate may consist largely of the artist's works.

---

[13] This discussion applies to estates of artists who at the time of death are U.S. citizens or residents and whose spouses (if any) are U.S. citizens or residents. Different rules apply in the case of nonresident aliens or if a surviving spouse is not a U.S. citizen.

Liquidity for the Small Estate
David Brown, Esq.

To assure sufficient funds for gathering and preservation of work, removal from premises, payment of normal debts, retention of estate counsel, etc., consideration should be given, if no other meaningful funds will be available, to low cost insurance.

Most savings banks provide low cost term life insurance. For example, the New York State Savings Bank Life Insurance cost for level term life insurance of $50,000 for a forty-year-old non-smoker male will remain at $332 annually for 15 years. Females generally pay a little less, and $25,000 life insurance is roughly a little more than half that cost. Therefore, for $50 to $75 every three months, there will be cash available to carry out the artist's basic wishes. Other states should have similar low cost insurance available.

If the estate, including the insurance proceeds, is likely to be less than $625,000, the artist's estate should be named the beneficiary of the policy. If adding the insurance proceeds to the artist's estate will cause the estate to exceed $625,000, the artist might consider gifting the policy to a trusted relative or friend, or to an insurance trust, so that the insurance proceeds will not be included in the artist's taxable estate and therefore the full amount of insurance proceeds (undiminished by estate taxes) would be available to be loaned by the relative/friend to the artist's estate as needed. Thus, should the artist become commercially better known and the value of his or her estate increase significantly, counsel should be asked for other suggestions for policy ownership or beneficiaries at that time which might result in savings on an estate where taxes were a consideration.

VALUATION[14]
Christina M. Baltz, Esq.

The valuation of an artist's assets is determinative of more than just the estate taxes payable on taxable estates. In the case of both taxable and nontaxable estates, the value given to the assets for estate tax purposes will be the income tax cost basis of the asset in the beneficiary's hands (the basis is said to be "stepped up" to the estate tax value). That is, if the beneficiary sells a work of art bequeathed to him by the artist, he will only pay capital gains tax on the amount (if any) by which the sales price exceeds the estate tax value of the work.

In the case of bequests to spouses, where no estate tax is imposed, it is therefore desirable to have a high estate tax value ascribed to the bequeathed assets. On the other hand, if an artist with a taxable estate is leaving property to persons other than a spouse, the potential capital gains tax advantage to the beneficiary of a high stepped up basis is counterbalanced by the higher estate tax to be paid by the artist's estate with respect to generously-valued assets. For taxable estates it is therefore generally desirable to have assets valued conservatively.

The estate tax value of an asset is its "fair market value" at the date of the artist's death (or as of the alternate valuation date, usually six months later, allowed under the Internal Revenue Code, if lower). For purposes of the estate tax, fair market value is defined as "the price at which the property would change hands between a willing buyer and a willing seller, neither being under any compulsion to buy or to sell and both having reasonable knowledge of relevant facts." The estate tax value is not to be determined by a forced sale price, and the sale price should be in the market in which the property would normally be sold (e.g., in the retail market versus wholesale market). The fair market value of the artwork may be established either by selling the artwork within a reason-

---

[14] This discussion applies to estates of artists who at the time of death are U.S. citizens or residents and whose spouses (if any) are U.S. citizens or residents. Different rules apply in the case of nonresident aliens or if a surviving spouse is not a U.S. citizen.

able period after death and using the gross sales price by having the artwork appraised.

Once the fair market value is determined, certain discounts can be applied to reduce that value (or premiums can be applied to increase the value) to determine the estate tax value. A "blockage discount" can be applied in the case of a large block of property. For example, the Federal estate tax regulations provide that, in the case of shares of stock, if the executor can show that the block of stock to be valued is "so large in relation to actual sales on the existing market that it could not be liquidated in a reasonable time without depressing the market" then the price at which the block could be sold outside the usual market may be used.

Although not set forth in the Internal Revenue Code or estate tax regulations, courts have allowed blockage discounts of 35% and 50% to be applied in determining the estate tax values for two well-established artists' very large bodies of work, recognizing that the artists' work would need to be sold over a considerable period of time in order to obtain what would be fair market value prices in the normal market for the artists' work. There are, however, no clear rules as to the percentage blockage discount (if any) that may be accepted in a particular case by the Internal Revenue Service (or a court, if the artist's estate disputes the estate tax value determined by the Internal Revenue Service).

Selling expenses, including commissions, are not automatically deductible and the Will must be carefully drafted to insure that the Internal Revenue Service will permit the estate tax deduction.

If the artist can successfully characterize his (or her) work as a business, other factors applicable to determining the net value of an interest in a business (e.g., future earning capacity of the enterprise) may be taken into account which could result in a lower value than a valuation of his artwork as tangible personal property owned by him at his death. In addition, if the artist's business can meet the requirements of the recently enacted "family-owned business exclusion", assets comprising the family-owned business of a value of up to $675,000[15] bequeathed to a "qualified heir" can be sheltered from Federal estate tax.[16]

It should be noted that a Federal estate tax return is required to be filed for an artist whose gross estate (i.e., all the artist's assets, not just the taxable estate) exceeds the exclusion amount, now $625,000 and gradually increasing to $1,000,000 in 2006. If the return reports "household or personal effects articles having marked artistic or intrinsic value" (which are defined in the estate tax regulations to include, among other things, paintings, etchings and engravings) which have a total value in excess of $3,000, then an appraisal prepared by an expert, under oath, must be filed with the return. In addition, any piece of art reported on the artist's estate tax return that has an appraised value at $20,000 or more must be submitted to the Internal Revenue Service's Art Advisory Panel for reevaluation. The Art Advisory Panel meets only twice a year and does not make public its evaluations.

---

[15] The $675,000 family-owned business exclusion is effective in 1998 is gradually adjusted downward to $300,000 in 2006 as the $600,000 unified credit amount referenced above is adjusted upward to $1,000,000, so that at all times the maximum amount sheltered from estate tax by reason of both is $1,300,000.

[16] Editor's comments. For a discussion of the valuation of an artist's enterprise as a business and qualification as a family-owned business for purposes of the estate tax exclusion, see Schaengold, D. Valuation of Artists' Estates: David Smith, Georgia O'Keeffe and Andy Warhol—"Have We Missed the Forest for the Trees?" 20 Tax Mgmt. Est., Gifts & Tr. J. 167, (Nov./Dec. 1995). But see 1965 IRS G.C.M. LEXIS, 176; G.C.M. 3402 rejecting the valuation of an artist's estate as a business in part because there is no indication in the art field of "inventory costs." Schaengold's proposal does not require legislative change. Franklin Feldman, co-author of Art Law: Rights and Liabilities of Creators and Collectors (Little, Brown, 1986), is currently circulating a legislative proposal to exclude artwork from the valuation of the artist's estate at death, and replace it with an inventory. When the estate or any beneficiary of the estate sold any of the work, the seller would be required to report the sale and pay ordinary income tax at the ordinary income tax rate (files of The Marie Walsh Sharpe Art Foundation).

THE APPRAISAL
Sylvia Leonard Wolf

It is important for an artist to have an inventory, or appraisal, prepared and up-dated during the course of the artist's lifetime for several reasons. The first is to record works created on an on-going basis, so that, in the event of a loss due to theft, fire, or water damage, a complete list can be submitted to substantiate an insurance claim. Such a list would be impossible to create from memory, after a disaster. The second reason to keep a well-prepared inventory is that it can be used to form the basis of a complete and accurate appraisal after death.

An appraisal is a statement of value, based on an analysis of the market in which an object is normally sold. Fair Market Value is the basis of appraisals made for Internal Revenue Service purposes, for estates, charitable gifts, gift tax donations, and estate planning. Estate appraisals also take into consideration a factor called blockage, which is based on the hypothetical supposition that all the works by that artist would be sold on his date of death. Fair Market Value derives from the presumed sale in the appropriate market for comparable items. This frequently, though not always, is the auction market. It could also be the dealer to dealer price.

The IRS does not accept retail gallery prices as fair market value, except in the case where that is the only venue for sales. The interpretation of the complexities of Fair Market Value has been the subject of many famous tax litigation cases of artists' estates. The estates of Andy Warhol, Robert Mapplethorpe, David Smith, Georgia O'Keeffe, Mark Rothko, and Willem de Kooning have all spent hundreds of thousands of dollars arguing in tax court, and with executors, and heirs, about the basis of valuation. At the very least, the artist, while alive, should prepare his own inventory, so that there is no dispute later as to authenticity, date, and medium of a specific work.

A properly prepared appraisal must include the following information:

- name of artist
- title of work and description of what it looks like
- medium
- size (height x width x depth)
- date
- signature and location
- condition
- bibliography, references, catalog number (if any)
- exhibition history
- photograph of the work

In addition, if the appraisal is prepared by someone other than the artist, or after his death, then it must also include:

- provenance (history of ownership)
- standing of the artist in his lifetime and at the time of the appraisal
- an analysis of his sales history
- the market at the time of the appraisal
- blockage discount

After considering all of the above, the appraiser must consider the quality of the work, within the context of the artist's oeuvre, and make a value judgement. This is the most difficult aspect of all, as it is often subjective, but at the same time, is based on an analysis of comparable sales of similar or like items. Works can be listed chronologically, if known, or by medium, and classified into A, B, C, etc. categories, based on prior sales history, and current sale potential.

CHECKLIST FOR ARTISTS' GIFTS OF ARTWORK:
A MUSEUM PERSPECTIVE
Beverly M. Wolff, Esq.

Introduction

Gift giving, to nonprofit institutions and to individuals, can be an effective element of "estate planning." The following outline discusses gifts and related planning issues relevant to visual artists.

Tax Restrictions on Charitable Contributions of Artwork by Artists

The artist is limited to an income tax deduction of his/her cost basis in the work if it is donated during the artist's lifetime. The artist will receive no income tax deduction if the artist leaves the work to a charity in a testamentary disposition.

Charitable contributions of artwork may benefit an artist's reputation, especially if the artist's works are accepted by a broad base of institutions, including institutions with good reputations and a large number of visitors. The earlier the artist makes such a gift, the sooner the artist is able to benefit from that boost to his/her reputation.

Arranging for Charitable Gifts

Artists wishing to give works of art to museums and other charities, during their lifetime or through a will, should contact the institution to discuss the gift. If the artist wishes to give to a museum, the artist should contact the appropriate curatorial department. If giving to another charity, the artist should contact the development office to learn the appropriate contact person with whom to discuss the gift.

Artists should be aware that many institutions receive far more offers of gifts than they can possibly accept. Also, a direct gift from an artist of the first work in a particular collection (as opposed to a purchase) may violate certain institutions' acquisition policies.

Upon learning that an organization is interested in the gift, the artist should arrange to give the work according to the institution's procedures. If the institution declines the gift, the artist should investigate other institutions that may be interested in such a gift.

Gifts to Charities Retaining Income

Artists can assist arts institutions in acquiring their artwork in ways other than outright gifts. Artists may wish to explore selling their work to charity on an installment plan or in exchange for an annuity or making a bargain sale (which is treated as part gift and part sale to the institution).[17]

They can give their artwork to charitable remainder trusts that will sell the work to the charity, and the purchase price will fund a trust that will pay a yearly income to the artist and his/her spouse. After both income beneficiaries have died, the charity will receive the remainder of the trust principal. Finally, artists can sell their work to a charity on an installment plan or in exchange for an annuity. If an artist exchanges work for an annuity from a charity he/she will receive a yearly annuity payment until his/her death. The annuity amount will depend on the valuation of the work at the time of donation and actuarial predictions of the artist's life expectancy.

Bequests

Most successful gifts of artwork to arts institutions have been arranged in advance by the artist and the appropriate curator. However, if the artist does not want to make his/her testamentary disposition known, he/she should have his/her will drafted to preserve the charitable gift. This can be done by providing an alternate recipient of the gift should the initial

---

[17] Comment. John Sare, Esq. From an income tax point of view, the annuity or bargain sale concept isn't necessarily attractive for artists, because their deduction is based on their basis. Gift annuity/bargain sale arrangements generally would be more attractive to a collector, at least for purposes of the charitable deduction.

donee decline it, and/or by granting the artist's executor the discretion to find an alternate charitable beneficiary should the initial institution decline the work.

Copyright Assignment and Licensing

An artist who does not have an heir to whom he/she would like to bequeath his/her copyright might consider transferring his/her copyright to an arts institution.[18] The institution would benefit from royalty earnings on the images and would be free to use the images to benefit the institution. Museums are usually happy to receive such a gift, but do not expect the copyright to be transferred with each work of art given to it.

Museums and other charitable institutions benefit greatly when artists grant them non-exclusive licenses to works of art that they give or sell to the institution. Such a license allows an institution to use the image to promote its collection and its educational purpose without any confusion over the need to clear rights or seek permission from the artist's heirs.

Non-Charitable Gifts

An artist may give any individual gifts of cash or artwork worth less than $10,000 in a year without incurring any gift taxes. A married artist may give up to $20,000 in any year without incurring taxes; the gift is assumed to come from both spouses. Beginning in 1997, the annual exclusion was indexed for inflation. It will increase in increments of $1,000 every two to four years (approximately) if the inflation rate remains at relatively low levels.

---

[18] Transfers of copyright interests by artists involve fairly intricate deductibility rules for the purposes of the gift and estate tax charitable deduction. See, Hoffman, *Copyright,* p. 82.

Gifts to Spouses

Property can pass between spouses during life, and at death, without incurring any transfer taxes. There is no advantage in transferring ownership of artwork to a spouse during an artist's lifetime, because the spouse will hold the property with all the same attributes as the artist.

The tax attributes of artwork change for the better when it is left to an artist's spouse through a testamentary disposition. The spouse receives a stepped-up basis in the artwork, equal to the market value on the date of the artist's death. The spouse will be able to sell the work, subject only to capital gains taxes on the appreciation of the artwork since the date of the artist's death. An artist's surviving spouse would also be able to donate the artwork to an arts institution and take an income tax deduction of the fair market value of the work on the date of the donation.[19]

Inventory

It is extremely important that an artist maintain an updated inventory of all the work he (or she) owns, has sold, and has given away. The inventory should include labeled slides of the work, consignment agreements, bills of sale, and deeds of gift.

The inventory will be significant in proving that particular works of art have left the artist's estate, and therefore, estate taxes on them are not due. The inventory will also insure that the heirs receive the works they were bequeathed, and that specific works of art are given to the correct recipients.

---

[19] So long as the art institution uses the artwork toward its exempt purpose and does not merely accept the work to sell it.

EXECUTOR'S OR ADMINISTRATOR'S CHECKLIST
Genevieve L. Fraiman, Esq.

The following checklist is not intended to be all-inclusive but to provide signposts that may assist an executor/personal representative in the administration of an estate.

Upon the death of the individual, the person named as executor under the will (or the relative or other person who intends to qualify as the administrator of the estate of a decedent who dies without a will) should:

1. Notify the family members of the death.

2. Search for the decedent's will, and possess the original will.

3. Review the terms of the will. If there are funeral instructions, promptly advise those making the arrangements. Obtain the names and addresses and relationships of the decedent's closest relatives who would be his distributees if there were no will (and the ages of any persons under 18 years of age, i.e., minors, and the names and addresses of the parent or other person with whom the minor resides). Obtain the names and addresses of all fiduciaries named in the will. Obtain the names and addresses of all devisees, legatees, and beneficiaries of trusts under the will (and the ages of any minors). Are any of the above who are adults under an incapacity?

4. Contact the decedent's attorney and retain that attorney (or another attorney) to obtain probate of the will and issuance of letters to the executor(s) and trustee(s) (or letters of administration if there is no will), to render legal advice in connection with the administration of the estate, and with respect to income, gift, estate, or generation-skipping transfer tax matters.

5. Contact the decedent's accountant who may have information regarding the decedent's financial matters. Obtain copies of the decedent's bank statements, custody account statements, all gift tax returns, and income tax returns for three full years prior to death.

6. Protect and inventory the tangible property, which may include obtaining the services of a security company and/or insuring the works of the deceased artist or his or her collection of the works of other artists. Obtain and review all of the catalogues, bills of sale, contracts, and any other records regarding the decedent's works of art. Are any out on loan? Are any being restored? Have any been sold on an installment basis? What contractual arrangements did the decedent-artist have with a gallery or dealer? Does the gallery or dealer have possession of any of the artist's works? Did the artist make any gifts of his or her works of art to family, friends or to museums or other charitable institutions during his or her lifetime? Were any of these gifts of fractional interests? Are there any outstanding promised gifts to museums or other charities of the artist's works that are enforceable at death?

Make a complete inventory of the artist's works on hand at his death. Keep records and make a list of all works of art disposed of by gift, sale, or otherwise prior to death.

Obtain independent appraisals of the decedent's works of art and other tangible personal property. Take 8x10 color photographs or 4x5 color transparencies of works of art with a value of $20,000 or more for submission to the IRS Art Advisory Panel.

Even if the estate will not be subject to Federal or state estate taxes, the works of art should be appraised to determine the stepped-up-to-date of death value for purposes of the capital gains tax that would be due when and if such work is sold by the estate or by the legatees or distributees.

If directed or authorized by the will, consider how best to continue the promotion of the works of art of the decedent, provided there are sufficient funds for this effort. Did the decedent create a foundation during his lifetime or direct or authorize the creation of a foundation in his will?

7. Obtain appraisals of the decedent's real property, condominium or cooperative apartment, closely held business, and any other asset that will be included in his or her estate (excluding cash and marketable securities). Obtain a valuation of the decedent's marketable securities.

8. Inventory all copyright interests and contractual agreements, if any, with respect to the artist's copyrights. When was each work created (fixed in a tangible form)? When does each copyright terminate? Were any works of the artist created as an employee? Did the artist assign or gift to others any copyright interests? Are copyright interests held by a trust, partnership, company or corporation? Have rights of termination been exercised by the artist before his or her death? During what time period, may the rights of termination be exercised by the artist's spouse or descendants? Calendar and make arrangements for protection of the artist's copyright interests. Notify the copyright office of the artist's death.

9. Inventory and collect the assets (including the items described in paragraphs 6 and 8 above) that will pass under the will ("probate assets"), which may include, among other things:

a. jewelry, household furniture and equipment, china, silver, linens, art, coins, stamps, automobiles, boats, and other tangible personal property

b. real estate (including a condominium) owned solely by the decedent or as a tenant in common

c. a cooperative apartment (including the shares of the landlord corporation and proprietary lease)

d. rights under a lease, including security given to the landlord

e. marketable securities

f. bank accounts

g. negotiable instruments that may include outstanding loans made by the decedent to others, and property securing such loans

h. closely held business interests (whether held as a sole proprietorship, partnership, limited liability company or corporation)

i. employee benefits and individual retirement accounts

j. insurance policies payable to the decedent or to his estate

k. assets held in a revocable trust created by the decedent that is payable to his or her estate at death

l. vested rights and powers of appointment of the decedent under the will or trusts created by others for the benefit of the decedent, or in the intestate estate of a pre-deceased parent or other relative.

m. club memberships

10. Inventory and obtain information concerning assets of the decedent that may pass outside of his or her will and may be included in the decedent's taxable estate, which may include, among other things:

a. joint bank accounts

b. trust bank accounts ("Totten trusts")

c. jointly owned real property, condominium, or cooperative apartment, owned as a tenant by the entireties with a spouse, or owned jointly with others.

d. joint custody accounts holding securities

e. insurance payable to named beneficiaries

f. employee benefits or retirement accounts payable to a spouse, children, or other named beneficiaries

g. trusts created by others in which the decedent had an interest (which may include a qualified terminable interest (QTIP) or power of appointment marital deduction trust created by the decedent's pre-deceased spouse)

h. revocable trusts created by the decedent, and payable or held in trust for others upon the death of the decedent

11. Obtain information concerning all unpaid bills and other debts owed by the decedent. After the will has been admitted to probate and letters issued to the executor/personal representative, debts that are legally enforceable should be paid.

12. Cancel all credit cards and accounts with stores, notify all banks, bro-

kers, businesses, magazines, clubs and other organizations of the decedent's death.

13. Notify the post office and arrange to have mail forwarded.

14. Notify social security.

15. Notify the insurance companies and arrange to collect the proceeds of the policies on behalf of the estate or named beneficiaries, and obtain the necessary tax forms provided by the insurance companies to be submitted with the estate tax returns.

16. If the decedent is survived by a spouse and/or minor children, ascertain what tangibles, automobiles and moneys, if any, that they may be entitled to as a family allowance. If the decedent left a will, will the surviving spouse exercise his or her right of election under section 5-1.1A of the New York Estates Powers and Trusts Law to take outright a pecuniary amount equal to the greater of: (i) the decedent's estate and testamentary substitutes up to $50,000, or (ii) one-third thereof.

17. If the decedent was living in a rented apartment, arrange to terminate the lease and to vacate the apartment.

18. Pay funeral and other administration expenses, or reserve funds for payment of the same.

19. Have the decedent's last income tax returns prepared and pay any taxes due.

20. Have prepared the Federal estate tax and any state inheritance, estate, or other death tax return due. If there are assets in a foreign country, it may be necessary to have prepared and to pay foreign death and other taxes due, and to review any estate tax treaties between the United States and the foreign country. Review the tax apportionment clause of the will and any applicable Federal and/or state apportionment statutes to ascertain who will bear the burden of estate and other death taxes. Pay any such taxes payable by the estate. Obtain a closing letter from the Internal Revenue Service and state tax authorities.

21. Manage the investments of the estate. In a large estate, it may be advisable to retain the services of an investment advisor and to maintain the securities in a bank or brokerage custody account in the name of the estate.

22. Carry out the terms of the will. Distribute specifically devised or bequeathed property, pay cash legacies, establish trusts created by the will. Distributions on account of the residuary estate before the final accounting of the fiduciaries may be considered, but a substantial reserve should be retained to meet unanticipated debts, expenses, or claims. The recipients of all payments and distributions are normally asked to sign a formal receipt and refunding agreement.

23. Do the terms of the will allow the executor or trustee to continue to promote the deceased artist's works? Who would benefit by and bear the expense of such promotion? Is such promotion feasible and practical?

24. Have prepared an account of all of the acts or omissions of the executor or administrator and the same settled judicially or informally by the execution of a receipt, release, and indemnification agreement. Make final payments of all outstanding debts (if any), administration expenses (including executor's or administrator's commissions and attorneys' fees), and make final distributions pursuant to the terms of the will (or to the distributees in the absence of a will).

Section 4-1.1 of the New York Estates, Powers and Trusts Law, provides for the distribution of property of a decedent not disposed of by will, as follows:

a. $50,000 and one-half of the residue to the spouse and the balance to issue by representation
b. if no issue, whole to the spouse
c. if no spouse, whole to the issue by representation
d. if no spouse or issue, whole to parent or parents
e. if no spouse, issue, or parents, to issue of parents by representation
f. if none of the above, one-half to maternal grandparents or if neither survives to their issue by representation, and one-half to paternal grandparents or if neither survives to their issue by representation.

ARTISTS' FOUNDATIONS

Christina M. Baltz, Esq., and Victoria Bjorklund, Esq.

An artist's private foundation can provide a vehicle for holding and managing an artist's art and enhancing the artist's reputation by promoting the public's interest in the artist's work. A private foundation is a tax-exempt entity and contributions to a foundation are eligible for income, estate or gift tax charitable deductions.[20] Because of the income, estate, or gift tax deductions available for gifts of art to a private foundation, creation of a private foundation may appear to be an attractive idea to an artist.

An artist cannot contribute his or her art to a private foundation and have the foundation merely hold the art; the foundation must be operated as an educational organization, offering a benefit to the public, to continue to qualify as a tax-exempt charitable organization under the Internal Revenue Code. Private foundations are subject to a relatively complex set of rules under the Internal Revenue Code and Treasury Regulations. In addition to the general rules applicable to private (grant making) foundations, an operating foundation, such as an artist's foundation, is subject to specific requirements with respect to using the foundation's assets, and paying out substantially all of its net income, to carry out its exempt purposes, and must demonstrate to the Internal Revenue Service annually that these requirements have been met.

Because of the income, estate, or gift tax deductions available for gifts of art to a private foundation, creation of a private foundation may appear

---

[20] Lifetime gifts of an artist's artwork to a private foundation are eligible for a Federal income tax deduction for the amount of the artist's cost basis in the work (essentially the cost of the materials used to create the work), but not for the amount of the fair market value of the work. The artist is entitled to a Federal gift tax deduction for the fair market value of the gifted work. In the case of a testamentary gift (i.e., made under the artist's will) of artwork to a private foundation, an artist's estate is entitled to a Federal estate tax deduction for the fair market value (at the artist's date of death) of artwork bequeathed to a private foundation. If instead of leaving the art to a private foundation under his or her will, the artist bequeathed the art to his or her spouse and the spouse then gifted the art to a private foundation, the spouse would be entitled to take a Federal income tax deduction for the fair market value of the gifted work.

to an artist to be an attractive idea. However, unless the artist's work is salable and can produce sufficient proceeds to sustain the operation of the private foundation, the artist or others will need to make cash contributions to fund the operations (e.g., rent, storage, insurance) of the foundation. Many artists assume that the foundation could engage in fundraising to derive support from the public. As a practical matter, however, this is an unlikely result for two reasons. First, grants are expensive and time-consuming to seek and only limited funds are available. Second, most grants are available from other private foundations and from corporations. For certain tax and policy reasons, most private foundations and corporations are much less likely to make grants to other private foundations than to public charities like schools or cultural organizations. Therefore, sales, admission fees, and licensing arrangements would be more likely sources of revenue, along with endowment income.

A common question is how much in cash or art assets is required to create a private foundation. As a legal matter, no minimum amount is required. As a practical matter, however, a private operating foundation may not be justified if the cash and assets are valued at less than $2 million. That is because private operating foundations can have high costs including rent, storage, insurance, and maintenance costs required for an art collection. In contrast, a private grantmaking foundation can be run for much less money, especially if its directors are willing to volunteer their time and talents. If services are not donated, accounting and filing fees may annually cost $5,000 or more. In either case, an artist should create a proposed budget in order to determine whether a private grantmaking or operating foundation makes sense given the artist's cash and art assets.

If the artist is not in a position to contribute the necessary funding and the proposed private foundation would be unlikely to be self-sustaining through sales of the art or fundraising, the artist should consider alternatives to establishing a private foundation such as the Archives of American Art (The Archives of American Art does not generally collect original works of art, but accepts sketch books, drawings, correspondence, diaries and oral histories) or a donor advised art fund for disposition of art (or its proceeds) to charity. Libraries of all sizes across the country represent a valuable resource for artists in placing their artwork and archival materials as do university libraries and art galleries. Regional and university museums may also prove to be an alternative to the artist's foundation.

An application to the Internal Revenue Service for recognition of tax-exempt status (called a Form 1023), in which the foundation must demonstrate how it is an educational organization benefitting the public and otherwise meets the requirements for tax exemption, must be filed with the Internal Revenue Service in order to obtain tax-exempt status. An artist does not need to wait to apply and receive confirmation of the foundation's tax-exempt status before making contributions to the foundation; if granted by the Internal Revenue Service, the foundation's exempt status will relate back to the date of its creation. Once established, the foundation will be required to file annual reports of its assets and expenditures (on Form 990PF) with the Internal Revenue Service.

In addition to complying with the rules and regulations and reporting requirements under the Internal Revenue Code, an artist's foundation may be required to register with the State Attorney General's office or other state agency charged with oversight of charitable organizations or fundraising activity within the state and also may be required to file annual reports with that state agency.

Assuming that the foregoing financial and regulatory hurdles to establishing the foundation can be met and the artist decides to form the foundation, he or she will need to decide whether to establish the foundation in trust or corporate form. A private foundation in trust form is established by a trust agreement between the artist, as settlor of the trust, and the trustee(s). Assets are transferred to the trustees to hold in trust and be administered or managed to carry out the foundation's exempt purposes in accordance with the terms of the trust agreement. The trust agreement generally may not be amended, but can be drawn broadly enough to give the trustees flexibility in operating the foundation. Other than the Internal Revenue Service and state filings described above, a private foundation in the form of a trust is not required to make regular filings with any governmental agency and the trustees are not required to appoint and formally authorize delegates to carry out the operations of the foundation.

A private foundation in corporate form is established by filing a certificate of incorporation with the Secretary of State of the state of incorporation and holding an organizational meeting at which the corporation's by-laws are adopted and the members (the non-profit corporation equivalent of shareholders) are named. In the case of an artist's foundation, the members would be the artist and any other person he or she wanted to share in the ultimate control of the foundation. After the organizational meeting, the members would hold their first meeting at which they elect the directors who are to manage the foundation, and the directors would then hold their first meeting at which they elect the officers who are to carry out the day-to-day operations of the foundation and formally authorize the officers to undertake certain activities necessary to carry out the foundation's exempt functions. Elections of directors and officers must take place annually thereafter. Under the corporation laws of most states, elections of officers and directors and board authorization of the officers' activities may be accomplished by unanimous written consent of the members or directors in lieu of holding meetings. The certificate of incorporation and by-laws may be amended by the members at any time (provided that the amended certificate of incorporation is filed with the Secretary of State). Annual filings and corporate franchise taxes may be required to be paid to the Secretary of State.

In general, the corporate form limits liability. It is more familiar to banks and businesses, while the trust may be less formal to operate. The directors of a corporation are generally judged under the business-judgment rule while trustees of a trust are held to higher fiduciary standards. The artist's legal advisor can explain in greater detail the differences between a corporation and a trust.

THE DOROTHY DEHNER FOUNDATION FOR THE VISUAL ARTS

In her will, Dorothy Dehner stipulated that all artworks of her own creation and 10% of her residuary estate should be given to a charitable non-profit foundation or organization. She requested that the Dorothy Dehner Foundation for the Visual Arts be formed, and named Joan Marter, art historian who had written a catalog and organized an exhibition of Dehner's as a director (before her death in 1994, Dehner had spoken to Marter about the ultimate disposition of her work, and Marter assured her of my willingness to serve as an "adviser").

The Foundation was organized in 1995, to support education in the visual arts with approximately one hundred ten thousand dollars and Dehner's artwork. Dehner's works have been donated to university art galleries and museums. Occasionally the Foundation has also supported an art historical publication which relates to Dehner and her contemporaries. Three directors or officers were named in Dehner's will, and additional directors have been selected by a vote of the original directors. Currently five directors serve, and were chosen because of their relationship to the artist and their positions as qualified advisers. All directors, including art historians, an artist, and a museum director, knew Dorothy Dehner personally. The Foundation's operating budget of forty thousand dollars annually is drawn from the funds transferred from the residuary estate, and the proceeds from sales of Dehner's works through commercial galleries. Monthly expenses include rental on storage facilities. Other charges are for conservation of works, purchase of photographs, and framing expenses as works are prepared for exhibition. The Foundation also gives grants totaling five thousand dollars annually.

Marter, who serves as the President of the Foundation, organized an exhibition entitled "Women in Abstract Expression" which included Dehner and arranged for the writing of a *catalogue raisonné* of Dehner's sculpture by a Yale University art historian. Marter has not received any pay for her services to the Foundation. Marter was also named as a successor executor and became executor on the resignation of the executor.

MAPPLETHORPE[21]

The director of the Mapplethorpe Foundation says that approximately two years before his death, Mapplethorpe and his lawyers established the general guidelines for the foundation, including areas he did not want to fund. Because he had assembled a trusted group of lawyers and friends, Mapplethorpe did not deal with the specifics beyond this level.

Mapplethorpe's dealer remains involved in most decisions concerning the sale and exhibition of work. The foundation director oversees all aspects of storing and preserving the archives, the bulk of which consists of unsigned black and white photographs stored in archival boxes at the foundation. Negatives have been put in notebooks which are kept in bank vaults located in a basement storage room in the foundation's office building. The framed work, as well as any unframed work signed by the artist, has been put in other art storage facilities. An in-depth inventory has been done to assess the condition of each work. There are three full-time staff members and three part-time employees, and the foundation sees no need for additional staffing.

It is unfortunate that this kind of well-run organization is not feasible for artists without assets of at least $2–3 million. Tina Summerlin, the foundation's director, recommends the following for dealing with the large number of less financially successful artists:

I would set up a volunteer advisory group of dealers, art consultants, auction experts and museum curators to look over a choice group of work from each artist involved, and then establish a specific level for each artist on a given scale of some sort, based on each artist's history. I would then work on a system of selling or dispersing work, trying to find as many diverse outlets as possible for each level of artist.

---

[21] Alliance for the Arts, *The Report of the Estate Project for Artists with AIDS* (1992) p. 30.

THE POLLOCK-KRASNER FOUNDATION
Ronald D. Spencer, Esq., Legal Counsel to the Foundation

The Pollock-Krasner Foundation was created in 1985 by the Trustees
of Lee Krasner, the widow of Jackson Pollock, pursuant to the instructions
contained in her will. The purpose of the Foundation, as set forth in the
will, is to furnish financial assistance to artists deemed by the Board of
Directors to be "needy and worthy." Krasner's two Trustees, Gerald
Dickler, a prominent art lawyer and longtime friend, and Eugene V. Thaw,
a distinguished art expert, private art dealer and co-author of the four-
volume *catalogue raisonné* of Pollock's work, were appointed by her will
as the Directors of the Foundation.

The Foundation was established as a Delaware not-for-profit corporation
and its office is located at 863 Park Avenue in New York City. The
Certificate of Incorporation of the Foundation gives Eugene V. Thaw the
sole authority for "marshalling, preserving, sale, loan, turning to account
and distribution" of all art owned by the Foundation. Gerald Dickler was
given sole authority for the administration of all other Foundation matters, including programs, staffing, and investments.

Under her will, Lee Krasner gifted the bulk of her estate, consisting of
financial assets and art created by her and her husband, to the
Foundation. Since the Foundation's creation the Foundation has sold much
of this art, utilizing the sales proceeds to fund its grants to artists. In its
twelve years of operation, the Foundation has made grants of almost
twenty million dollars to more than 1,500 artists in sixty-three countries.

The staff of the Foundation reviews applications and conducts financial
investigations to determine the financial circumstances of the applicants.
An anonymous and distinguished Committee of Selection meets regularly
to review the slides presented by artist applicants to determine artistic
merit.

The success of the Foundation is due in large part to its simplicity of purpose—providing grants to individual working visual artists of established
ability who demonstrate financial need. Its success is also a function of

its simplicity of governance and management—two Directors, each expert in their respective fields, art and law, advised by a Committee of Selection and aided by a small and efficient staff overseen by an Executive Vice President, Charles C. Bergman, an expert in the administration of foundations.

THE ANDY WARHOL FOUNDATION FOR THE VISUAL ARTS, INC.
Peter McN. Gates, Esq., Counsel to the Warhol Foundation

Andy Warhol died on February 22, 1987. His will left substantially all of his estate to a charitable foundation to be formed by his executor having as its purpose "the advancement of the visual arts." The Andy Warhol Foundation for the Visual Arts, Inc., was established on May 1, 1987. Pursuant to the will, the initial directors of the Foundation were Andy Warhol's brother and two of the artist's closest associates. The Board is now a fully independent body which includes museum professionals and others active in the art world, as well as businessmen and financial professionals. Archibald Gillies has been President of the Foundation since 1990.

Andy Warhol left an extraordinary estate. In addition to many other assets (including "collectibles" which sold at Sotheby's for over $25 million) his estate included over 100,000 of his own paintings, drawings, prints, and photographs, over 100 films he created, 4,000 hours of video footage, and hundreds of boxes of stored archival material. All of these assets had to be analyzed, inventoried, preserved, stored, insured, and appraised, an immensely complex, time-consuming, and costly project, which continues to this day. A major task has been, and continues to be, the conversion of the Foundation's Warhol art to cash as rapidly as the marketplace permits. In effect, the Foundation has had to operate a major art business. This activity will continue for many more years.

The Estate and the Foundation have also had to devote substantial time and resources to defending, successfully, against unfounded claims and lawsuits, including a claim by the attorney hired by the Estate for legal fees of $16 million (the final award was a fraction of the claim).

While dealing with these problems, the Foundation has actively pursued its purpose of advancing the visual arts. It joined in creating the Andy Warhol Museum in Pittsburgh, donating over 3,000 of the finest works in the collection, and the film and video collection, and providing cash support, has placed over 100 major works in 24 museums through a program of deeply discounted sales, and has made over 800 cash grants totaling more than $24 million.

COPYRIGHT AND OTHER INTELLECTUAL PROPERTY ISSUES
IN ESTATE PLANNING AND ADMINISTRATION FOR THE VISUAL ARTIST
Barbara Hoffman, Esq.[22]

One of the most valuable assets of the visual artist and his or her estate—second only to the artist's artistic property—may be the right to control and manage the exploitation of the rights which are incorporated under the rubric of "intellectual property." For the visual artist, the most important intellectual property right is copyright.[23]

Control of the reproduction of their copyrighted images has long been a concern of photographers and their estates.[24] The traditional art reproduction market for the creator of original works of fine art was posters, postcards, the occasional T-shirt, and art books. Recently, the growth of the multimedia industry, with its voracious appetite for the visual image, the licensing of works of fine art in film and television and the explosion of art image merchandising—Picasso watches and towels, Calder umbrellas, puzzles of well-known images, for example, Ringgold's Tar beach, Norman Rockwell suspenders[25]—increases the importance of careful management of copyright by the visual artist during his or her lifetime and in the planning of his or her estate for both economic and artist rights/reputational reasons.

---

[22] ©Barbara Hoffman 1998

[23] Trademark law offers less protection to the visual artist who creates unique works of authorship, because of the standard for infringement—consumer confusion—and the need in some cases to prove secondary meaning. For example, Andy Warhol's estate could not prevail on a trademark infringement claim against the publisher of a calendar that reproduced Warhol's works when Warhol had sold works without retaining copyrights and the calendar disclaimed endorsement by the Warhol estate. Artists who sell work in volume as in the form of posters or calendars are more likely to receive trademark protection.

[24] For example, the Estate of Dianne Arbus is well known for its review and control over the content of text which accompanies a license to use an image of her work. Generally in the visual arts, art historians are all too familiar with the concept of the "widow censor."

[25] The Norman Rockwell Museum in Massachusetts proposes 1,200 different items, from mugs to trouser suspenders—incorporating images in whole or in part from Rockwell's prints and paintings.

This chapter explores the basic considerations that should be taken into account with respect to the creation, exploitation and preservation of artistic and intellectual property with special concern to copyright issues in the planning and administration of the visual artist's estate. Also included are sample clauses to incorporate in estate planning documents dealing with the disposition and control of artistic and intellectual property.

Copyright Basics[26]

"The source of Congress' power to enact copyright laws is Article I, cl. 8, of the Constitution. According to this provision, 'Congress shall have Power . . . To promote the Progress of Science and useful Arts, by securing for limited Times to Authors . . . the exclusive Right to their respective Writings.'"

To be protected under current U.S. copyright law, a work "must be an original work of authorship fixed in a tangible medium of expression."[27] The Copyright Act imposes no requirement of aesthetic merit as a condition of protection. However, a work must have "at least some minimal degree of creativity." Works of visual art—a painting, a photograph, a sculpture—are protected by copyright. Thus, the simple act of creating an original work in a "fixed" medium including the electronic, gives the author copyright in the work. Under Section 106 of the Copyright Act of 1976 (the "Act"), the copyright owner has the exclusive right to (1) reproduce the work in copies or phonorecords, (2) prepare derivative works based on the copyrighted work (which includes the right to recast, transform or modify), (3) distribute copies by sale or other ownership transfer, or to rent, lease, or lend copies, (4) perform the work publicly, (5) display the work publicly. For certain one-of-a-kind visual works of art and num-

---

[26] More detailed copyright information as well as a copyright registration form VA is found in the Appendix.

[27] The current U.S. law known as the Copyright Act of 1976 became effective on January 1, 1978. All works of art created before that date are governed by the Copyright Act of 1909.

bered limited signed editions of two hundred copies, authors (artists) have the right to claim authorship (attribution) and prevent the use of their names in conjunction with certain modifications of the works and the right to prevent alteration of their work (integrity). (Section 106A.) The latter two rights—known as *droit moral* or moral rights–sourced in the protection of the author's personality, receive limited protection in the U.S. scheme of copyright based on the author's economic rights. France, Germany, Italy, and Japan are strong moral rights countries. For example, under French law, after the death of an artist, an heir or designee by will is given authority to assert the artist's "moral rights," including the right to authenticate which works are done by the artist. The holder of the moral right may act to prevent a reproduction of particularly poor quality which distorts the work; or a reproduction of good quality which is marketed in a context injurious to the nature of the work or the artist's personality.

Ownership of the bundle of intangible rights comprising copyright is separate and distinct from ownership in the work of art. Under current law, absent a writing expressly conveying copyright, the sale, gift, or transfer of the original work of art does not transfer the copyright in the work of art. Under the 1976 Act, copyright interests can be transferred inter vivos or at death and in whole or in part.[28] For example, a copyright owner can transfer all the rights or one or more of the exclusive rights or a full or undivided interest, or a divided interest in the copyright. A copyright owner may divide copyright in the work in a number of ways: by the type of use and/or media, by an exclusive license or non-exclusive license, by territory or duration, to name only a few possibilities.

---

[28] Under the 1976 Act, as a result of poor drafting, it is arguable that intervivos transfers of copyright are treated differently from testamentary dispositions. Under section 201(d), the latter subject is state law will and trust formalities. Section 201(d)(2) suggests that testamentary transfers are restricted to indivisibility. Paul Goldstein, *Copyright,* 2 ed., Little Brown, 1996, ß4.4.2., p. 4:56.

At least since the passage of the current law, it is no longer customary for a museum when purchasing an original work of art from an artist to require an artist to convey copyright to the work of art as a condition of the purchase.[29] Most museums request the artist convey to the museum a non-exclusive license to use the artwork for standard museum practices. A non-exclusive license is not a transfer of copyright ownership, but a transfer of a contract right; thus, the museum cannot bring a copyright infringement action. A form used by The Museum of Modern Art is enclosed at the end of this section. Both non-exclusive and exclusive licenses are usually negotiated to reflect the artistic, economic, income, gift and estate tax interests of the artist and the museum.

The 1976 Copyright Act vests initial ownership of copyright in the creator of the work unless it is a work for hire. The 1909 Copyright Act prescribed a term of copyright measured by twenty-eight years from the date of the work's first publication; the copyright term could be renewed once for a second twenty-eight year term. Ownership of works created under the 1909 Act will be determined under the 1909 Act rather than the 1976 Act. The 1976 Copyright Act provides as a general rule that the term of copyright in a work created on or after January 1, 1978, begins with the work's creation and ends fifty years after the death of the work's author. The 1976 Act also extends the duration of any copyright that has in its renewal term or was registered for renewal between December 31, 1976, and December 31, 1977, to a term measured by seventy-five years from the date the copyright was originally secured.

---

[29] Under section 201(d)(1) of the Copyright Act, the author of a work may, as the initial owner of the copyright, transfer copyright by transferring in writing all rights in the work. "All rights, in or to the copyright in the work." Caveat: It is not clear that the testamentary phrase "I give and bequeath all right, title and interest in my Self Portrait" without mention of copyright transfers the copyright. Testamentary as well as intervivos transfers of copyright should explicitly state that copyright is being conveyed. The holder of an exclusive license is treated like any other owner of a copyright interest, and may bring infringement actions.

Artistic Property, Copyright and the Artist's Estate Plan

Copyright and other intellectual property rights should be specifically discussed and addressed in any visual artist's estate plan. Although there is no one correct solution, unified management of both artistic and intellectual property may in certain situations be a desirable course of action.

If an artist dies intestate or if both artistic property and copyright pass as part of the artist's residuary estate to more than one beneficiary, there may be difficulty in agreeing on a single course of action for the artist's work; particularly if there is discord among the beneficiaries. This is similarly true for copyright, where if copyright passed to multiple beneficiaries under the artist's will, or by the laws of intestacy, the beneficiaries would each own the copyright as joint owners either as tenants in common, joint tenants, or community property depending upon applicable state law.[30]

Copyright Law and Its Intersection with the Income, Gift, and Estate Tax[31]

Sections 170(f), 2055(e)(2), and 2522(c)(2) of the 1954 code disallowed a charitable deduction for income, estate, or gift tax purposes, respectively, where the donor transfered an interest in property to a charity (e.g., a remainder) while also either retaining an interest in that property (e.g., an income interest) or transferring an interest in that property to a non-charity for less than full and adequate consideration subject to certain limited exceptions.[32]

---

[30] A discussion of the rules of copyright joint ownership is beyond the scope of this paper. Generally both the rights and liabilities of "co-owners" under both the 1909 and 1976 Act parallel that of real property tenants in common. The rules, however, may be varied by contract.

[31] This is an extremely complex and intricate area. A full discussion of the income, gift, and estate tax consequences of transactions in artistic and intellectual property, including the different consequences of gift, sale, license, and non-exclusive licenses is beyond the scope of this article, but should not be overlooked by the estate planner or administrator of the estate.

The restrictions on deductibility of split interest transfers to charity were added by the Tax Reform Act of 1969 to insure that there was a reasonable correlation between the amount of the charitable deduction and the value of the property received by charity. The rules provided by the Congress to accomplish this result disallowed the charitable deduction if interests in the same property were transferred for both charitable and non-charitable purposes unless the charitable interest was in certain specified forms.

In 1981, as a result of the passage of the Copyright Act of 1976, and the changes in the copyright law which treat the tangible object (i.e., the original artwork) and the intangible copyright as separate items of property, Congress amended the gift and estate tax laws. The Joint Committee Report stated "these two items of property typically are not transferred together. Moreover, the use or exploitation of the artwork or copyright generally does not affect the value of the other property. As a result, it will be possible to determine the value of the tangible object (i.e., the original artwork) apart from its related copyright interest by reference to values of similar objects which are sold without their copyright interest. Accordingly, the value of the artwork which is used to determine the amount of the charitable deduction should provide a high degree of correlation with the value of property received by charity. See 17 U.S.C. @ 102."

The Congress concluded, therefore, that the disallowance rule for transfers of split interests in property should not apply to a work of art and the related copyright in cases where the work of art but not the copyright is transferred to charity and where there are restrictions to insure that the public will benefit from the transfer. However, the Congress believed that this rule should apply only for estate and gift tax purposes and not for income tax purposes.

---

[32] Exceptions to this general rule are provided for: (1) remainder interests in charitable remainder annuity trusts, charitable remainder unitrusts, pooled income funds, farms, and personal residences; (2) present interests in the form of guaranteed annuity or a fixed percentage of the annual value of the property; (3) an undivided portion of the donor's entire interest in the property; and (4) a qualified conservation easement.

The Joint Committee Report then stated:

"Thus, the provisions of the Act allow gifts and bequests of works of art for the benefit of the general public without imposition of tax, but do not provide the unnecessary tax incentive that could occur if the provision were extended to the income tax."

Thus, currently, if a donor or decedent makes a qualified contribution of a copyrightable work of art to a qualified organization, the work of art and its copyright are treated as separate properties for purposes of the estate and gift tax charitable deductions. Thus, a charitable deduction generally is allowable for the transfer to charity of a work of art, whether or not the copyright itself is simultaneously transferred to the charitable organization if the use of the work of art by the charitable organization is related to the purpose and function constituting its basis for exemption. If the artist bequeaths a sculpture to the museum without conveying the copyright on condition that the work be exhibited as part of its permanent collection, he or she receives the deduction.[33] If the artist instead bequeaths the artwork without the copyright to the Buddhist Center Hospital, the artist will not get the deduction, unless the artist can establish a related use.

Under the income tax regulations, an artwork and its copyright are not treated as two distinct properties, as they are under Federal copyright law, and for estate and gift tax purposes. Thus, the gift of an artwork without its copyright to a museum does not qualify for a charitable deduction. The failure to qualify for a charitable deduction results from treatment of contributions of artwork without the copyright as gifts of a partial interest. Generally, unless a contribution falls within one of the limited statutory exceptions to the partial interest rules, only gifts of complete interests will entitle the donor to a deduction under Section 170. For example, a deduction is not allowable for the value of an immediate and perpetual gift not in trust of an interest in original historic

---

[33] Most museums do not like to accept restricted gifts. General museum practices are at variance, therefore, with the restrictions for deductibility imposed by the Federal gift and estate tax laws.

motion picture films to a charitable organization where the donor retains the exclusive right to make reproductions of such films and to exploit such reproductions commercially. Regs. Sections 20.2055-2(e)(1)(ii), 25.2522(c)-3(c)(1)(ii); Sections 2055(e)(4), 2522(c)(3). Compare Regs. Section 1.170A-7(b)(1)(i) which addresses the partial interest rules.

Regulation ß20.2055-2(e)(2) provides two examples:

Example (1). A, an artist, died in 1983. A work of art created by A and the copyright interest in that work of art were included in A's estate. Under the terms of A's will, the work of art is transferred to X's charity, the only charitable beneficiary under A's will. X has no suitable use for the work of art and sells it. It is determined under the rules of ß 1.170A-4(b)(3) that the property is put to an unrelated use by X charity. Therefore, the rule of paragraph (e)(1)(ii)(a), which treats works of art and their copyrights as separate properties, does not apply because the transfer of the work of art to X is not a qualified contribution. To determine whether paragraph (e)(1)(i) of this section applies to disallow a deduction under section 2055, it must be determined which interests are treated as passing to X under local law.

(i) If under local law A's will is treated as fully transferring both the work of art and the copyright interest to X, then paragraph (e)(1)(i) of this section does not apply to disallow a deduction under section 2055 for the value of the work of art and the copyright interest.

(ii) If under local law A's will is treated as transferring only the work of art to X, and the copyright interest is treated as part of the residue of the estate, no deduction is allowable under section 2055 to A's estate for the value of the work of art because the transfer of the work of art is not a qualified contribution and paragraph (e)(1)(i) of this section applies to disallow the deduction.

Example (2). B, a collector of art, purchased a work of art from an artist who retained the copyright interest. B died in 1983. Under the terms of B's will the work of art is given to Y charity. Since B did not own the copyright interest, paragraph (e)(1)(i) of this section does not apply to disallow a deduction under section 2055 for the value of the work of art, regardless of whether or not the contribution is a qualified contribution under paragraph (e)(1)(ii) (c) of this section.

From a purely tax point of view, the artist is faced with the unenviable position should he or she decide to make a lifetime gift of a work of art to a museum—of being denied an income tax deduction unless the artist donates the copyright in the work of art along with the work of art—and then his or her deduction will only be equal to the cost of materials.

Will Bumping

Estate law and copyright law collide in another area—what has been called "will bumping." The controlling statute is section 17 U.S.C. 304(a) of the Copyright Law which establishes priorities with regard to the right to renew the copyright and thus ownership of the copyright during the renewal term. To the extent that an artist's assets include copyright interests, including renewal interests, the artist's testamentary freedom may be restricted. The problem only exists for works of art created between 1970 and 1978. A full discussion of the potential for conflict and strategy or steps an intellectual property lawyer or estate planner can take to deal with it are discussed fully in an excellent article: Francis M. Nevis, Jr., "The Magic Kingdom of Will Bumping," 35 *Journal of the Copyright Society of the U.S.A.*, 2, 77, 110 (1988). While works created after January 1, 1978, will not include a renewal term and are not subject to will bumping, certain restrictions on the artist's freedom of transfer are created by Section 203 which gives authors and their statutory successors the nonwaivable right to terminate copyright grants after the lapse of a prescribed period. Section 203 does not apply, however, to testamentary grants.

Valuation of Copyright and Other Intellectual Property for Estate Tax Purposes

Copyright and other intellectual property interests are included in the gross estate of an artist. Although as with the tangible property, these intangible rights are difficult to measure, in some cases, they may be a significant wealth transfer to the estate, with a resulting tax liability. Cost, selling price, sales of comparable properties, cost of reproduction and expert opinion may all be relevant in valuation. A court has recognized that an artist/testator may decrease the value of intellectual property in his or her estate by devising an estate plan to transform those assets prior to distribution. Caveat: The restrictions must be imposed by the artist testator, not the beneficiaries who receive the property.[34]

Collecting Societies

Collecting societies administer the copyrights and intellectual property rights of visual artists and photographers in much the same way as ASCAP and BMI. Two visual artists societies are VAGA, located at 521 Fifth Avenue, New York, New York 10026, (212) 808-0616 and Artists Rights Society, 65 Bleecker Street, New York, New York 10012, (212) 420-9160. These societies also represent the interests of European collecting societies in the U.S. The current use of collecting societies in the fine arts is less widespread than in the photography or music industry. Many visual artists currently elect to monitor and manage their own intellectual property. For example, the Picasso estate, which was formerly with A.R.S., now manages its own intellectual property. In the photography field there has been formed a subsidiary of the ASMP for the purpose of

---

[34] In dictum, the court explained that the estate tax is a "tax on the privilege of passing on property, not a tax on the privilege of receiving property." Therefore, as the court stated:
The valuation should . . . take into account transformations brought about by those aspects of the estate plan which go into effect logically prior to the distribution of property in the gross estate to the beneficiaries. Thus, for example, if a public figure ordered his executor to shred and burn his papers, and then to turn the ashes over to a newspaper, the value to be counted would be the value of the ashes, rather than the papers.

facilitating the electronic licensing of rights and photographs. The basic purpose is to have 5,000 of the world's best photographers with millions of images accessible through a single transaction through this subsidiary.

Some Thoughts on a Checklist for Copyright and Intellectual Property Management in Estate Planning and Administration

1. Inventory copyright interests and other intellectual property assets; record all assignments, exclusive licenses, non-exclusive licenses.

2. Create art image and likeness usage checklist for prospective licensees/usages.

3. Plan for unified management of artistic and intellectual property and identify future owners of artistic property, secondary materials like journals, photographs, letters and copyright interests in both categories.

4. Consider various options for copyright licensing management.

5. Consider moral rights (statutory and contract).

6. Create documents for foundation, trust, basic licensing forms, artist/gallery consignment agreements.

7. Seek out and enter into agreements with art critics, art historians or galleries for preparation of *catalogue raisonné* of all or part of a body of work.

8. Provide testamentary instructions and guidance concerning copyright exploitation of works of art in the estate.

9. Consider limiting value in the estate plan by imposing restrictions on the use of intellectual property.

WILL CLAUSES FOR THE VISUAL ARTIST, WITH SPECIFIC EMPHASIS ON CENTRALIZED MANAGEMENT OF ARTISTIC PROPERTY AND COPYRIGHT INTERESTS[35]

Barbara Hoffman, Esq.

Caveat: The following will clauses are illustrative only and should not be used without an understanding of the relationship of a clause to the overall estate plan.

Clause Devising Personal Property of the Artist to his or her own Charitable Foundation.

An artist may wish to contribute secondary materials to his or her private foundation or an art trust. The foundation or trust can be created by the artist prior to death or by testamentary directive. Note that separate documents, apart from the will, are necessary to create a not for profit foundation or trust which are governed by state law. The exempt status of the organization is governed by Federal law.

_____ I give, devise and bequeath my tangible personal property other than works of art, as follows:

A. To the Foundation:

1. All of my business and personal papers, including, without limitation, letters written to or by me, dairies, journals, memos and all other writings of every nature and description, together with all copyrights thereon and the rights of publication thereto.

2. All photographs, polaroids, video tapes, films, video and audio cassettes made by me or dealing with me and/or my work.

---

35 © Barbara Hoffman 1998

3. All catalogues, books, magazines and other writings dealing with me and/or my work or made by me, together with all of those items of memorabilia, clothing, furniture and objects which were painted on or decorated by me and which my Executors deem, in their sole and absolute discretion, to be of significant value or interest.

Residuary Clause giving art and copyright interests to Artist's foundation with clauses creating the Foundation[36]

_____ I give, devise and bequeath all of the rest, residue and remainder of my estate, of whatsoever kind and nature, whether real or personal and wheresoever situated, which I may own or to which I may be entitled at the time of my death, including, without limitation, works of art created or owned by me and not otherwise bequeathed pursuant to any other provisions of this Will, together with any copyrights relating thereto, any other rights of any kind, including but not limited to trademarks and rights of publicity, lapsed legacies and all property over which I may have any power of appointment, to the Foundation, a non-profit, charitable and educational foundation created or which shall be created under the laws of the State of New York, provided that such organization or institution shall be an organization described in both Section 170(c) and 2055(a) of the Internal Revenue Code of 1986, as amended, or any corresponding section of any tax law in the United States from time to time in effect. The initial Board of Directors of the Foundation shall consist of _____,
_____, _____ and _____. I further direct that _____ shall also serve as Executive Director of the Foundation, at a fair and appropriate salary, to supervise the work and purposes of the Foundation.

---

[36] See chapter on Artists' Foundations and the importance of funding the Foundation or Trust.

The purposes of the Foundation shall include, but shall not be limited to, the following objects and purposes:

(1) To distribute property and grants to institutions, such as museums or schools which will exhibit and/or make artworks created by me available for viewing and study by art historical scholars and/or by the general public;

(2) To perpetuate the understanding of works created by me, through publication of reproductions of my writings, drawings, paintings or other works in the form of books, films, or video tapes, as the Foundation sees fit.

I hereby direct that my Foundation distribute a portion of any earned income which it generates to the following charitable organizations: . . . . The Foundation shall have complete discretion to decide if, when and how often any distributions may be made. The Foundation shall further reserve the right to ensure that the use of any funds is being properly handled and may request proof of such usage.

I enjoin the Board of Directors of the Foundation to remain true to the ideals and charitable intentions that I have followed and which I have shared with them.[37]

Clause Devising Artist's Personal Property to Charitable Institution, other than Artist's Foundation.

Caution: It is critical that an artist testator specify that the bequest to a charitable organization is to be put to a designated charitable purpose if the copyright work is not conveyed with the artwork.

---

[37] More specific language and guidance might be appropriate to guide the Board of Directors.

_____ I give all photographs, prints, negatives and other photographic material owned by me at my death, not otherwise specifically bequeathed herein, to such charitable organizations or institutions as shall be selected by my Executor provided that each such organization or institution shall be an organization described in both Section 170(c) and 2055(a) of the Internal Revenue Code of 1954, as amended (or any corresponding section of any tax laws of the United States from time to time in effect) and provided that such charitable institutions are willing to comply with the conditions and restrictions which my executor may impose including the manner and frequency of exhibition of these materials and their availability for study and research.[38]

Clause Terminating Gallery and Centralizing Management of Artistic and Intellectual Property

_____A. I direct my Executors to gather together and inventory all of the works of art created and/or owned by me at the time of my death. To the extent possible and where not barred by contracts and/or agreements then in effect, they shall take back for the benefit of my estate all such works out on consignment to art dealers or galleries or on loan to museums, organizations and individuals and all maquettes and models that may be stored or held at fabricators, publishers and galleries.

This direction is intended to include all works of art created by me which were on consignment for sale or otherwise in the hands of various art dealers and galleries, including my primary art dealer and including all works which have not then been sold or, if sold, have not yet been paid for and payment is past due.

---

[38] The Artist, while alive, should attempt to identify the museum or university who will receive his or her personal papers and other property. Many museums will not accept bequests of personal papers. An alternative should always be provided.

B. I direct my Executors and/or the Board of Directors of my Foundation to carry out any licensing and grant of reproduction rights of my artwork as they, in their sole discretion, may determine. It is my hope, however, that they will do so as they believe I would have done and in a way that will retain the original impact and integrity of the imagery.

Clause Providing That Executor Consult with Professional Advisor

If the testator wishes to appoint an executor or trustee who is not experienced in dealing with art or intellectual property as an asset, one option would be for the testator to provide in the will that the executor or trustee should consult with a professional dealer or agent when managing such assets. An example of language providing for this arrangement follows:

I direct my Executor [or Trustee] to consult with _____ prior to exercising any powers granted to my Executor [or Trustee] with respect to [describe the artistic property subject to this clause]. My Executor [or Trustee] shall not be liable to any person if my Executor [or Trustee] acts in reliance upon or in accordance with the advice of _____ in connection with the management of [describe artistic property].

Another option is to appoint the professional who is familiar with the art market, art and copyright, and intellectual property matters as an executor, co-executor or trustee and/or successor executor or trustee. In such case it is necessary to recognize and explicitly name conflict of interest concerns.

Clause Waiving Conflict of Interest

I have appointed as fiduciaries persons with whom I presently have business associations. _____, my designated executor and trustee, has served me as my attorney for more than ten (10) years and has served with great distinction. She is far more familiar than any other individual with my business activities and with my wishes with respect to the disposition of works of art which I have created as well as with respect to works created by others which I have collected. She is a specialist in the law of intellectual and artistic properties as well and a close and trusted personal friend.

I recognize that, in their fiduciary capacities, my fiduciaries may transact business with entities in which they have a personal interest. I have complete confidence in the integrity of the fiduciaries I have designated in this will and authorize them as fiduciaries to transact any business they deem appropriate with themselves and/or with any business entity with which they may be associated, notwithstanding any actual or potential conflicts of interest which might arise. In the event that any person acting as a fiduciary hereunder shall enter into any transaction in which there are or could be actual or potential conflicts of interest, she shall not be required to seek court approval and shall be under no greater duty of care and no greater constraint in any respect than she would have been if she had engaged in a similar transaction at arm's length with any unrelated party.

Clause Giving Trustee Power to Manage Copyright Property

Normally, the documents creating the inter vivos or testamentary trust enumerate the powers to be given to the trustee. If a copyright is to be included in a trust, the following language may be included in the list of powers given to the testamentary trustee:

To copyright or renew any copyright of any copyrightable work; to exploit in such manner as the Trustee shall determine, in the sole discretion of the Trustee, any such copyright and to authorize the use of such part or all of any copyrightable work, or any rights arising by any reason of any copyright, in such manner as the Trustee, in the Trustee's sole discretion, shall determine.

DEED OF PARTIAL GIFT TO THE NATIONAL GALLERY OF ART

On this the _____ day of _____, 199___, I, _____, hereby give to the Trustees of the National Gallery of Art ("the Gallery") absolute and uncon-ditional ownership of an undivided _____ percent of my right, title and interest in an original sculpture created by me ("the work") together with all copyright and associated rights which I have therein. The Gallery shall be entitled to possession of the work for a total of _____ days out of each calendar year. The undersigned shall be entitled to possession of the work for the balance of each calendar year.

I wish that the work be identified in the permanent records of the Gallery, and when on exhibition, as a partial and promised gift of _____.

I hereby promise to give the balance of my remaining _____ percent right, title and interest in the work to the Gallery not later than by bequest in my last will and testament. Until then, while the work is in my possession, I will make adequate provision for its care and security and will keep the Gallery apprised of its location. The Gallery will have the right to inspect the work peri-odically, at mutually agreeable times, to check on its condition.

It is my understanding that the Gallery's insurance will cover the fraction of the work owned by the Gallery while the work is in my possession and will cover the entire value of the work while the work is at the Gallery and in transit to and from the Gallery.

Before agreeing to lend the work or authorize its reproduction, I agree to notify the Gallery of my intentions and to obtain its concurrence as co-owner of the work.

DATE:_____   DONOR:_____

Address of Donor: Telephone:

I certify that a deed of gift and the subject thereof were physically present in the National Gallery of Art prior to the meeting of the Trustees of the National Gallery of Art on _____ at which meeting the Trustees accepted the gift as described above.

Secretary

NON-EXCLUSIVE LICENSE[39]

I, _____, the undersigned, being the owner of the copyright in and to _____ (describe the artwork),[40] created by me, and desiring to further the purposes of The Museum of Modern Art, New York, do hereby, by way of gift, authorize The Museum of Modern Art to reproduce copies of said work, to distribute reproductions of said work to the public, to transmit[41] or otherwise communicate a display of said work to a place open to the public or to the public by means of any device or process (examples include but are not limited to slides, film and television), whether the members of the public capable of receiving the display receive it in the same place or in separate places and at the same time or at different times, and to authorize others to do the same, BUT ONLY ON CONDITION THAT all copies of said work bear a copyright notice as prescribed by the Copyright Law of the United States.

This non-exclusive license, which does not transfer ownership of my copyright to the Museum of Modern Art, shall endure for the entire term of the copyright in and to said work and shall survive all assignments of copyright.

_____   _____
Date   Signature of Artist

---

[39] The income, gift, and estate tax implications of this license are beyond the scope of this chapter.

[40] Different restrictions may be appropriate to negotiate for different media.

[41] New licenses are currently being developed for licensing of artwork by the artist creator in the new media and by museums in connection with the licensing of their existing collections.

CONFLICT OF INTEREST ISSUES IN ESTATE PLANNING FOR VISUAL ARTISTS

Erik J. Stapper, Esq.

In considering the appointment of a fiduciary, whether executor or trustee, and the selection of a qualified attorney, the artist must be cognizant of the many opportunities for conflicts of interest. The most obvious conflict situation for an artist arises when the artist selects his or her dealer or publisher as one of the fiduciaries. The tension between earning commissions on the sale of artwork and planning for the long-term welfare of either the artist's survivors or the body of work left behind has led to litigation. Perhaps the most well-known example of self dealing and breach of fiduciary obligation is Matter of Rothko. "A fiduciary faced by a problem of conflict of interest should not use his dual position to deal for his own self-interest." The executors of Rothko's estate which included a director of the Marlborough gallery and an artist represented by the gallery agreed to sell paintings to Marlborough Gallery with a fifty-percent commission, unless the paintings were sold to or through other dealers, in which case the commission was to be forty percent. Several of the contract terms were questionable, including the inflated commission (paintings sold during Rothko's lifetime through Marlborough had earned only a ten-percent commission), interest-free installment payments over a twelve-year period, and the sale of so many paintings within a short period of time. Thus, the appointment of the dealer as the executor may have the unintended effect of preventing the person most familiar with marketing the artist's work from continuing to do so.

There are, however, many less obvious cases of conflict which can be easily overlooked. The following scenarios and the attached checklist are not meant to be all-inclusive. They are, however, intended to serve as reminders to the artist who begins to think about an estate plan that one or more individuals or institutions must take over when the artist's death or incapacity terminates a career and that those persons may have a conflict of interest in carrying out their fiduciary duties. A conflict can be waived after it has been fully disclosed. Moreover, if the scenarios or multiplicity of cautions here appear overwhelming, the artist must keep in mind the costs and burdens on survivors, whoever they may be, if there is no estate plan (his or her estate goes to the family members specified by law).

1. Selection of spouse, non-marital partner or close friend

If the proposed fiduciary, whether spouse, non-marital partner or close friend, is also an artist, the appointment may have the effect of forcing that appointee to choose between pursuing his or her own artistic career and preserving and advancing the work of the deceased artist. Conversely, if the devoted spouse or acolyte is not an artist, the testator must consider whether there will be a significant financial burden placed on the fiduciary for which the estate's after-tax assets may not be sufficient. Consider for a moment the cost of storing, insuring or otherwise maintaining the body of artwork left behind. This burden will be very different, of course, if the artist is a miniaturist or a creator of giant sculptures.

2. Selection of other family members

The selection of one person as fiduciary may be more efficient than the naming of several persons because no time is lost to reach agreement between co-fiduciaries. In large or complicated estates, co-fiduciaries may be desired, particularly where each can perform well on her expertise in separate or specific tasks. To do so may create hurt feelings between the artist's surviving children or siblings. An even more difficult situation is created if there is a surviving spouse or non-marital partner who is not the parent of the child selected as fiduciary. This tension becomes extremely high when the child is forced to select assets that will make up the marital deduction property for a step-parent. For instance, who gets the artwork or other non-income producing assets and who receives the cash and securities? What will the survivor live on?

Even without remarriage family relations change as the result of intervening deaths. A fiduciary who could work well with the artist's surviving siblings may not be effective when that sibling predeceases the artist so that the fiduciary must now deal with nieces and nephews or their spouses or their children.

3. Selection of attorney to prepare estate plan

In addition to being satisfied with the attorney's competence as an estate planner, the artist must find the fee arrangements acceptable.[42] The question of fees should be raised at the earliest possible moment, for instance, in the telephone call making the initial appointment. Will that first visit result in a fee even if the attorney is not the one the artist uses for the estate plan? Will the fee be based only on time spent or is there a maximum? Is there a minimum? If the fee is a fixed amount how many drafts or rewrites are possible? What eventualities will change the fee estimate or fixed amount? What disbursements will be charged to the artist?

In addition to the estate planning fee now, the artist must find out on what fee basis the attorney or law firm will attend to the legal work needed to administer the estate. THERE IS NO REQUIREMENT THAT THE FIDU-CIARY EMPLOY THE LAWYER WHO DRAFTED THE WILL. Therefore an agreement to reduce estate planning fees in exchange for being the estate's attorney restricts the executor's discretion and may lead to a difficult working relationship between them.

If a bank is appointed executor,[43] it is not unusual for the bank to use the drafter of the will as the estate attorney. If there are two executors each coexecutor can hire his or her own attorney, but the total fees cannot exceed the fee that would have been payable to one attorney. In the

---

[42] The New York State Administrative Board of the Courts has approved a Statement of Client's Rights that must be posted conspicuously in lawyers' offices throughout New York beginning in 1998. [See Appendix A]

[43] It is every New York bank's practice to use the drafter of the will as the estate's attorney unless there are very unusual circumstances (making an error in the will is not such a circumstance).

two attorney case the lawyers must divide the work in a manner acceptable to both executors. For instance, one firm prepares the probate
papers and collects or identifies the assets and the other firm prepares
the estate tax returns and the estate's fiduciary income tax returns.

Will the bank in gratitude for receiving the will appointment agree to a
higher legal fee than otherwise? Therefore the artist should discuss the
question of billing for estate work with the attorney at the time the
estate plan is made even though it is impossible to fix the post-mortem
fee in advance. The purpose of the question is to find out on what basis
the fee will be determined, for instance, a percentage of the estate, and if
so, how is the estate valued for this purpose (probate estate v. Federal
gross estate). If the fee is to be based on time charges the artist should
ask for written confirmation of the current hourly rates so that the executor can verify that any subsequent increases merely cover inflation or
other factors as well.

If a fixed fee is offered the artist must again find out what legal services
are included in the fee and which items will be extra, for instance, the
artist's final income tax returns. A fee that is based on a percentage of
the estate's value creates a conflict between the beneficiaries' wish to
keep a valuation low for estate tax purposes and the attorney seeing a
fee increase from a higher valuation. This in turn raises a question about
how an appraiser is selected since the appraiser's work product can
increase legal fees.

4. Selection of attorney as fiduciary

At one time it was not unusual for some attorneys to advise their clients
that only an attorney could be an executor (in some instances the advice
was for two attorneys). This unethical practice is now contrary to a specific provision added in 1995 to the New York State Surrogate's Court
Procedure Act. This new provision, Section 2307-a, requires a New York
attorney to disclose to all estate planning clients that, subject to limited
statutory exceptions, any person, including an attorney, is eligible to

serve as executor. Moreover, the attorney must disclose that any person, including an attorney, is entitled to receive a statutory commission. The disclosure must include an explanation that the statutory fee is payable in the absence of an agreement to the contrary. Finally, the attorney must disclose to the client that the attorney who is named as executor will also be entitled, or an affiliated attorney will be entitled, to receive just and reasonable compensation for legal services. This is usually referred to as "double dipping."

Most importantly, the client must confirm the attorney's disclosure in a signed writing. In the absence of the required written acknowledgment, the attorney's commission as executor is limited to one-half the statutory amount.

To some extent the statutory disclosure is not sufficient because it does not require a disclosure of how the statutory commission is calculated in New York State.[44] The commission is based on the executor receiving and paying out all sums of money, including income earned during administration and on the commission paid out. Property that the executor never receives is not included in the computation even if part of the taxable estate. Examples include retirement benefits, life insurance, or joint accounts that go to named persons and not to the estate (in New York an "in trust for" designation avoids inclusion of a bank account in the "probate" estate as a result of a decision in Matter of Totten leading to these accounts usually being referred to as Totten Trusts). A joint account can become part of the probate estate if it can be established that the joint account was used for the convenience of the decedent and not as a "testamentary substitute."

---

[44] The statutory amount now in effect is calculated as follows on commissionable assets:

5% of the first	$ 100,000
4% of the next	200,000
3% of the next	700,000
2 1/2% of the next	4,000,000
2% of the excess over	5,000,000

Also not included in the commission calculation base is property specifically identified, or a fixed amount, that is given in the will to a named person, a "specific legacy," and not as part of the balance of the estate referred to as the "residuary estate." Real estate is not included in the calculation even if it is part of the residuary estate, unless the executor is required to take action regarding the property, such as removal of title problems (a "cloud on title"), evicting tenants, or partitioning the property among several beneficiaries of the residuary estate.

Another problem in calculating commissions comes up when the artist is the beneficiary of a trust established by a predeceased spouse, parent, or grandparent and the artist can designate who is to receive the trust assets at the artist's death, a "power of appointment." Frequently such powers can be used to pay estate taxes. If the power merely directs payment of the tax to the government, that amount does not become part of the calculation base. If it is directed to be paid to the executor for the purpose of having the executor pay the estate tax, then the amount so received and paid out may be included in the calculation.

5. Selection of other professional advisers

The problem of selecting an appraiser who is independent of the attorney has already been mentioned. Conflicts can also arise between beneficiaries where gifts of artwork are equalized or supplemented by cash legacies. Similarly, if the will provides for an allocation of estate taxes, a conflict can be created among beneficiaries.

CONFLICT OF INTEREST CHECKLIST
Erik J. Stapper, Esq.

Conflicts to Be Considered in Making an Estate Plan
Selection of fiduciaries:

1. Naming of attorney and disclosure requirements. Is the New York mandated disclosure sufficient? Is it enough to state that fee is fixed by statute and is the same for whoever serves as fiduciary? No, Section 2307 of the Surrogate's Procedure Act specifically states that the statutory fees apply "absent an agreement to the contrary."

> a. Coexecutors.

> b. Statutory fee (e.) amount specified in will.

> c. Calculation of commissions and exclusions from base, for instance, real estate and specific legacies unless work is required.

> d. Power to retain experts and the source of their fees. Do they reduce commissions or are they an additional charge?

> e. How to pay for the estate plan. Is the will appointment intended to compensate the planner for the planning and other legal services?

2. Naming of unrelated professional such as bank, accountant, financial advisor, business associates (curator).

> a. Since the designated fiduciary must eventually approve the legal fees for administration of the estate, is there a relationship between estate planner and designated fiduciary that may lead to approval of unwarranted fees?

b. Planner's estate plan may have the effect of minimizing or maximizing the executor's commission through use or non-use of specific legacies, a decision that can affect fiduciary's attitude toward legal fee to be approved.

3. Naming of family member.

a. Effect on family relations when only one sibling is named to gain efficiency.

b. Inefficiency of administration when naming multiple executors.

c. Relationship between surviving spouse and stepchild fiduciary especially when funding marital deduction.

d. Relationship between fiduciary and heirs of predeceased sibling.

e. Relationship between heirs and fiduciary who is sibling of the deceased.

f. Discretionary selection by fiduciary of tangible personal property to satisfy specific legacy.

g. Problems are magnified for estate of visual artist who leaves behind a collection of artwork because of valuation problems and sentimental attachments; order of selection.

h. Listing of these problems may discourage decision making.

i. Non-traditional family.

Some Potential Conflicts in Administering the Estate

1. Selection of counsel and fixing of legal fees.

   a. Does not have to be the drafter of the will.

   b. Percentage of estate
      i. Probate estate
      ii. Federal gross estate
      iii. Valuation

   c. Time charges and disclosure of hourly rates.

   d. Fixed fee.

   e. Description of services that are included in a fee agreement and what is additional.

2. Selection of appraiser

   a. International auction house v. independent appraiser.

   b. Fee for appraisal.

   c. Limitations on appraisal, including disclosure of intended uses.

   d. The Art Advisory Panel of the Commissioner of Internal Revenue.

   e. Revenue Procedure 96-15, 1996-1 Cum. Bull. 627 for advance valuations that apply for income, estate, and gift tax purposes.

   f. Conflict of interest between executor and counsel toward beneficiaries and appraisal decision.

g. Conflict of interest between fiduciaries and counsel and appraisal decisions.

h. Conflict of interest between beneficiaries where cash is bequeathed to equalize property bequests or where income tax basis becomes an issue.

i. Change positions when second death occurs during proceeding.

3. Tax allocation clauses for non-charitable legacies and conflict between beneficiaries as to values.

CONFLICT OF INTEREST DISCLOSURE FORM

The following are the statutory models of the testator's written acknowledgment of an attorney's disclosure of who can serve as executor:

(a) When set forth in writing executed prior to or concurrently with a will:

Prior to signing my will, I was informed that:

(i) subject to limited statutory exceptions, any person, including an attorney, is eligible to serve as my executor;

(ii) absent an agreement to the contrary, any person, including an attorney, who serves as an executor for me is entitled to receive statutory commissions for executorial services rendered to my estate;

(iii) if such attorney serves as my executor, and he or she or another attorney affiliated with such attorney renders legal services in connection with the executor's official duties, he or she is entitled to receive just and reasonable compensation for those legal services, in addition to the commissions to which an executor is entitled.

_____   _____

(Witness)   (Testator)
Dated: Dated:

(b) When set forth in a writing executed subsequently to the will:

I,   , have designated my attorney,
[a] [an] [executor] [alternative executor] [coexecutor] (delete what is inapplicable) in my will dated

Prior to signing my will, I was informed that:

(i) subject to limited statutory exceptions, any person, including an attorney, is eligible to serve as my executor;

(ii) absent an agreement to the contrary, any person, including an attorney, who serves as an executor for me is entitled to receive statutory commissions for executorial services rendered to my estate;

(iii) if such attorney serves as my executor, and he or she or another attorney affiliated with such attorney renders legal services in connection with the executor's official duties, he or she is entitled to receive just and reasonable compensation for those legal services, in addition to the commissions to which an executor is entitled.

_____   _____

(Witness)   (Testator)
Dated: Dated:

1997 CHANGES IN ESTATE AND GIFT TAX LAWS AND THE VISUAL ARTIST

Erik J. Stapper, Esq.

1997 was a year in which the estate and gift tax provisions of both the Internal Revenue Code and the New York State Tax Law were changed. The New York State change is in fact a repeal and will be reviewed first because it also provides an insight into the operation of the Federal law.

New York State Estate Tax Law

In calculating the Federal estate tax the Internal Revenue Code allows a credit for a specified amount of state estate tax. Therefore many States and the District of Columbia adopted an estate tax that is exactly equal to the amount of the Federal credit. By doing so these jurisdictions did not increase the total estate tax burden because in the absence of the state tax the Federal tax would be greater by the same amount. Therefore this type of estate tax is usually referred to as a "sop tax" because it sops up the Federal credit and taxes nothing more. Moreover, when there is no Federal tax due because the estate does not exceed the federally exempted amount there is no state estate tax and no state return filing requirement.

New York, however, imposes its own separate gift and estate taxes beginning at $115,000. The New York estate tax rates exceed the allowable Federal estate tax credit at all levels (the maximum New York state tax rate is 21 percent and the maximum Federal credit rate is 16 percent). More significantly, there is no Federal credit for gift taxes paid to a state so that there is no relief from the New York gift tax other than to move to a sop tax state, such as Florida.

New York has now enacted a sop tax for estates of decedents dying on or after February 1, 2000. The New York gift tax is repealed for gifts made on or after January 1, 2000. Until then the New York gift and estate taxes will remain in effect except that the exemption will increase from $115,000 to

$300,000 for decedent's dying on or after October 1, 1998, and for gifts made on or after January 1, 1999. The non-parallel transition treatment by New York of its gift and estate taxes is a trap for the unwary. The simplest plan is to defer making gifts of $300,000 to 1999 and all larger gifts until the year 2000.

Internal Revenue Code

The most frequently discussed change and the question that all artists will ask is whether their estates will qualify for the family-owned business exclusion of new Section 2033A as added to the Internal Revenue Code by the Taxpayer Relief Act of 1997 (signed into law on August 5, 1997, making it the "date of enactment"). The provision is effective for estates of decedents dying after December 31, 1997. It is a complex provision and before dealing with it, other important changes should be considered first even though they may be of more general applications.

Revaluation of gifts

Section 2001(f) has been added to prevent the Internal Revenue Service from revaluing for estate tax purposes lifetime gifts for which the limitations period has passed. The effect of such a revaluation had been to redetermine the applicable estate tax bracket and available unified credit.[45] The revaluation problem was of particular concern for gifts of works of art or interests in family businesses. The change is effective for gifts made after the date of enactment (8/5/97).

---

[45] The revaluation did not result in an additional gift tax liability because the return years were closed. The revaluation had the effect, for example, of using up more of the $600,000 exemption or pushing the estate into a higher estate tax bracket. This change can be correctly described as a taxpayer relief provision.

Gift tax exclusion

The annual $10,000 gift tax exclusion has been indexed for inflation effective for gifts made after December 31, 1998, based on the 1997 calendar year.

Increase in estate tax exemption

The much heralded increase of the estate tax exemption to $1,000,000 has been accomplished technically by adding to the Code the term "the applicable credit." It is defined to be the amount of the tentative tax computed on the "applicable exclusion amount."

The 1997 changes did not index the $1,000,000 exemption for inflation in years after 2006. It also did not change the unified estate and gift tax rate. At $1,000,000 that rate is 41 percent. It reaches the maximum rate of 55 percent at $3,000,000.

Estate tax deferral for business assets

Existing law allowed in effect for a complete five-year deferral for the payment of estate taxes and a partial deferral for 14 years by having no payments, other than interest, for the first four years and then installments of principal and interest over the next ten years to the extent the tax is attributable to a closely held business. The value of that business must exceed 35 percent of the adjusted gross estate. [46] Moreover, Section 6601(j) provides that the tax attributable to $400,000 of that value qualifies for a special 4 percent interest rate. In addition, the entire amount of interest, including the 4 percent amount, paid on the deferral is deductible in recalculating the estate tax initially determined to be due.

The deferral provisions have been revised to eliminate both the estate and income tax deduction for the interest. In exchange for the loss of the deduction of the interest payment, the 4 percent rate has been reduced

---

[46] There has been no change in the eligibility requirements for the installment election.

to 2 percent and the amount of tax that qualifies for the 2 percent rate ("the 2 percent portion") is the tax attributable to $1,000,000 (an amount indexed for inflation after 1997) of closely held business assets regardless of the excluded amount.[47] More importantly, the tax attributable to the business assets that is in excess of the 2 percent portion will bear interest at an amount equal to 45 percent of the applicable interest rate. These changes are effective for estates of decedents dying after December 31, 1997. A special election is provided for existing installment agreements.

Judicial review of installment payment eligibility

If the Service determines that an estate is not eligible[48] for installment payments, that adverse decision can now be brought before the Tax Court in a declaratory judgement action. The change is effective for estates of decedents dying after the date of enactment (August 5, 1997). Previously there was no judicial relief because the Tax Court only had jurisdiction over "amounts" in controversy.

Exclusion for family-owned business

After December 31, 1997, a new section will exclude from an estate the "adjusted value of the qualified family-owned business interest of the decedent." The excluded amount cannot exceed $1,300,000 less the applicable exclusion amount. Thus by 2006 the amount of the exclusion will only be $300,000. For 1998 it is $675,000 ($1,300,000 less $625,000).

---

47 Before this change the amount of tax attributable to $1,000,000 of such business assets had to be calculated by taking into account the $600,000 exemption. Consequently, the old law applied only to $400,000 of small business assets.

48 Continuing eligibility for installment treatment that had been initially allowed but is being denied in a later year is also covered by the declaratory judgment provision.

In considering whether to elect the new family-owned business exclusion the executor and the family must be conscious of the possibility that when artwork is sold as part of an ongoing family business profitable sales, measured by reference to date of death values, may produce ordinary income which may then also be subject to the self-employment tax. If the election is not made, the profit may qualify for capital gain treatment. In this connection it is important to note that gain on the sale of "collectibles" remains subject to the 28 percent capital gains tax (or 15 percent if that is the applicable bracket). The term "collectible" means "any work of art" regardless of how acquired or who created it.

GLOSSARY
Barbara Hoffman, Esq.

Accounting. The preparation of financial statements that will give the court, the beneficiaries, and everyone involved in the estate a clear picture of the property in the estate available for distribution, and a history of the transactions dating back to the time the executor first took control of the property. An accounting may be formal or informal. The beneficiaries review the accounting and their approval of the accounting releases the executor for liability arising from his or her activities as executor.

Administration. The management of the estate of a deceased person. It includes collecting the assets, paying the debts and taxes, and making distribution to the persons entitled to the decedent's property.

Administrator (m); Administratrix (f). The person appointed by the court to manage an estate if the decedent had no valid will or if the will did not provide for an executor or executrix.

Advance valuation of art. A revenue procedure that allows a taxpayer to obtain from the Internal Revenue Service a Statement of Value for certain art contributed to a qualified charitable organization. Under the revenue procedure, a taxpayer's request for a Statement of Value from the Service must be made before the taxpayer files the Federal income tax return on which such a contribution is first claimed as a deduction under Section 170 of the Internal Revenue Code. The revenue procedure requires the taxpayer requesting a Statement of Value to pay a user fee. A taxpayer may rely upon the Statement of Value in completing his or her tax return (i.e., it is binding and the IRS may not dispute the claimed value).

Alternate value date. For Federal estate tax purposes, the value of the gross estate six months after the date of death, unless property is distributed, sold, exchanged, or otherwise disposed of within six months. In that case, the value of such property is determined as of the date of disposition.

Annual exclusion. Gifts made in a given calendar year are taxable minus the allowable exclusions and exemptions. The Federal gift tax exclusions are (i) the annual exclusion and (ii) amounts paid on behalf of another person for certain educational expenses and for medical care. The annual exclusion permits $10,000 in gifts to each separate recipient each year or $20,000 if a husband and wife elect to split the gift.

Art Advisory Panel. The Internal Revenue Service in 1968 created a panel consisting of nationally prominent art dealers, art professors, art museum directors and art advisors to assist in the valuation of appraisals of artwork or cultural property with a claimed value for tax purposes of twenty thousand dollars or more. The Panel meets in Washington, D.C. usually once or twice a year at closed meetings in each speciality area. The determinations of the Art Advisory Panel, in practice, become the position of the Internal Revenue Service.

Assets. In probate law, the property—real, personal, tangible, intangible, legal, and equitable—of a decedent available for the payment of debts and legacies.

Audit. Tax audits by Federal and state authorities are adversarial, with the government attempting to raise the largest tax possible and the taxpayer trying to pay the least allowed by law.

Beneficiary. The person who inherits a share or part of the decedent's estate; one who receives a beneficial interest under a trust, insurance policy, or retirement plan.

Bequest. A gift of personal property by will, as distinguished from a gift of real property. A specific bequest is a gift of specified property. "I give to my studio assistant Leonardo, an original artwork entitled 'Self Portrait,' 1996." A general bequest is one that may be satisfied from the general assets of the estate. "I give $100 to my studio assistant, Francois Picasso." If the specific bequest was sold before the decedent died, the gift will fail.

Blockage discount. Valuing artwork in an artist's or collector's estate is a central issue of estate planning. *Estate of David Smith* is a landmark case which established the application of the principle of a blockage discount to works of art, previously developed in stock evaluation cases. In *Smith*, the court allowed a blockage discount involving the works of David Smith, recognizing the "impact of simultaneous availability of an extremely large number of items of the same general category." Cases involving the *Estate of Georgia O' Keeffe, The Estate of Andy Warhol* and *The Estate of Robert Mapplethorpe* have further developed the concept. Blockage is not only a relevant concept in determining the value of an artist's estate for Federal estate tax purposes. The concept is also applied in determining the executor's fees, distribution and the beneficiaries, basis in the property for the purposes of determining gain or loss on subsequent sale.

Buy/sell agreement. Also called a business agreement. An arrangement for the disposition of a business interest in the event of the owner's death, disability, or retirement or on the owner's withdrawal from the business at some earlier time. Business purchase agreements take various forms: (1) an agreement between the business itself and the individual owners (a stock redemption agreement); (2) an agreement between the individual owners (cross/purchase agreement); and (3) an agreement between the individual owners and a key person, family member, or outside individual (a third-party business-buyout agreement).

Capital gain property. Any property the sale of which at its fair market value at the time of the contribution would have resulted in long-term capital gain. The property is a capital gain property if it has appreciated in value and, beginning January 1, 1998, if it has been held by the donor for more than one year, unless owned by the artist who created it. [Section 1221(3).]

Charitable organization. A trust or non-profit organization exempt from Federal income tax under IRC § 501(c)(3) is popularly referred to as a charitable organization. Charitable organizations are characterized as either public or private. Public charities generally receive part of their support from the general public. They include churches, schools, hospitals, museums, and other publicly supported organizations. Private operating foundations, certain organizations operated in connection with another public organization, and those private foundations that distribute all their receipts each year may be deemed public charities for certain purposes, including the Federal tax treatment of charitable contributions. Private charities include all other exempt organizations, and include the usual kind of private foundations. It is important to verify the status of the charitable organization as either a public or a private charity when making charitable contributions as the public or private status determines the charitable deduction limitation applied to the contribution.

Charitable remainder annuity trust. A trust that permits payment of a fixed amount annually to a noncharitable beneficiary, with the remainder going to charity.

Charitable remainder trust. An irrevocable trust that pays income to one or more noncharitable beneficiaries for a period of years or for life, then pays the remainder over to a designated charity. In order to qualify for the charitable income, gift, or estate tax deductions the trust must take the form of an annuity trust or a unitrust.

Charitable remainder unitrust. A trust designed to permit payment of a variable annuity (i.e., a fixed percentage of the trust's assets as revalued year by year) to a noncharitable beneficiary, with the remainder going to charity.

Code: The Internal Revenue Code. The Code includes Federal income, estate, and gift taxation provisions.

Codicil. A supplement to an existing will to effect some revision, change, or modification. A codicil must meet the same requirements regarding execution and validity as a will.

Common disaster. An accident that results in the simultaneous death of both the decedent and the intended beneficiary.

Community property. Property acquired during marriage in which both husband and wife have an undivided one-half interest, therefore, not more than half of the assets of the community can be disposed of by the will of either spouse. There are currently eight community-property states: Arizona, California, Idaho, Louisiana, Nevada, New Mexico, Texas, and Washington.

Contingent interest. A future interest in real or personal property that depends on the fulfillment of a stated condition that may never come into existence. "I give and bequeath my studio at Arles to my brother Theo, if he becomes a painter."

Contingent remainder. A future interest in property dependent on the fulfillment of a stated condition before the termination of a prior estate. For example, Pablo Picasso leaves property to a bank in trust to pay the income to Françoise during her lifetime. After her death, the trustee is to transfer the property to the decedent's son, Paolo, if the son is then living; otherwise, it goes to his daughter, Paloma. Paolo has a contingent remainder interest—contingent upon his outliving his mother. Paloma has a contingent remainder interest, which she will receive only if the son does not outlive the mother.

Copyright. A bundle of intangible property rights created by law which include the right to control the reproduction, distribution, public performance and display, and to prepare derivative works based on the work. To be protected under current U.S. copyright law, a work "must be an original work of authorship fixed in a tangible medium of expression." Works of visual art—a painting, a photograph, a sculpture—are protected by copyright.

Corpus. The principal, as distinguished from the income. When we speak of the corpus of a trust, we are talking about the assets in the trust (versus the income generated by those assets).

Decedent. The person who died (whether man or woman).

Descent. The passing of real estate to the heirs of one who dies without a will.

Devise. A gift of real estate under a will, as distinguished from a gift of personal property.

Disclaimer. A renunciation or refusal by a beneficiary of his or her right to accept an obligation or interest in property. Disclaimers are used effectively as a postmortem estate planning tool.

Distribution. The passing of personal property to the heirs of one who dies without a will. Also, the formal act of the executor in disposing of the estate's assets to the designated beneficiaries.

Domicile. An individual's permanent home. The place to which, regardless of where he or she is living, an individual intends to return. Domicile is an important concept in estate (and income tax) planning. The validity of a will is determined by the testator's domicile at death. The decedent's domicile at death determines the state that will tax the estate other than real property and certain tangible property located outside the state. Objective criteria such as voting history, income tax payments, memberships, and licenses when combined with statements and declarations of the client's intent, determine domicile. Artists with multiple studios and residences in the U.S. and abroad should consider the estate and other tax consequences of domicile.

Donee. A person or entity who receives a gift.

Donor. A person or entity who makes a gift.

Escheat. In the absence of lawful heirs, and subject to the claims of creditors, the property of a person dying intestate is said to escheat—that is, to "return" to the state.

Estate tax. A tax imposed on the right of a person to transfer property at death. The tax is imposed not only by the Federal government but also by various states. "For the purposes of the [estate] tax imposed by the Code, the value of the taxable estate shall be determined by deducting from the value of the gross estate the amount of all bequests . . . to or for the use of any . . . charitable [purposes]." [2055(a)(2).]

Executor (m); Executrix (f). The person named by the deceased in his or her will to manage the decedent's affairs; the personal representative of the decedent who stands in the shoes of the decedent, collects the assets of the estate, pays the debts and taxes, and makes the distribution of the remaining property to the beneficiaries or heirs.

Fair market value. The value at which estate property is included in the gross estate for Federal estate tax purposes; the price at which property would change hands between a willing buyer and a willing seller, neither being under compulsion to buy or sell and both having knowledge of the relevant facts. The Treasury regulations define fair market value for artworks sold at public auction, as the auction price plus buyer's commission [TAM9235005]. Currently, selling expenses, including commissions, are not deducted from fair market value for estate tax purposes unless required to meet estate obligations and expenses.

Family Limited Partnership. A Family Limited Partnership ("FLP") is created under state law by an FLP Agreement. Generally, when a donor makes a gift, the donor must give up all future control over the gifted property. In an FLP the donor contributes property to the FLP in exchange for general and limited partnerships interests. By retaining the General Partnership interests and making gifts of the Limited Partnership interests, the donor, in effect, retains control over the gifted property. Artwork may be an appropriate asset to transfer because of its appreciation potential.

Fiduciary. One who occupies a position of trust. Executors, administrators, trustees, guardians, attorneys, and accountants, all stand in a fiduciary relationship to persons whose affairs they are handling. As such, they must avoid all conflicts of interest and owe a duty of loyalty to the estate. An executor of an artist's estate who was an artist, under contract with galleries to which paintings in the estate were sold or consigned has a conflict of interest resulting from the advantage he might gain in the purchase and sale of his own paintings. Similarly, an executor of an artist's estate who was a director and officer of one or two related art galleries to which paintings in the estate were sold or consigned has a conflict of interest through inducements to favor the galleries' interests, including the aggrandizement of his status and financial advantage through sales of his family's private art collection.

Generation-skipping transfer tax (GSTT). A flat-rate tax imposed in addition to the Federal gift or estate tax, and at the highest current estate or gift tax rate, on transfers to "skip persons" (essentially transfers to grandchildren). The GST tax may be imposed on direct skips (such as when a grandparent writes a check to a grandchild) or where property passes from one generation to another in less obvious ways by trust or otherwise. There is a $10,000 per donee (or $20,000 if the gift is made by husband and wife) annual exclusion from GST tax similar to the annual exclusion from Federal gift tax.

Gift. A gratuitous transfer of property. To be considered a gift, the transfer is complete when it leaves the person who makes the gift and the person (donor) retains no power to change the disposition of the property either for her own or another's benefit. The elements of a gift under New York law are: donative intent, delivery, and acceptance.

Gift tax. A tax imposed on the lifetime gratuitous transfer of property. In addition to the Federal gift tax, some states also impose a tax on transfers during lifetime.

Gift-tax exclusion. For Federal gift-tax purposes, anyone, married or single, can give up to $10,000 in cash or other property each year to any number of persons (whether or not they are related to the donor) with no gift-tax liability. The exclusion is doubled to $20,000 in the case of a married donor whose spouse consents to split the gift. (Note: also referred to as the annual exclusion.)

Grantor. A person who creates a trust; also called a settlor, creator, donor, or trustor.

Gross estate. The value of all property owned by the decedent or in which the decedent had an interest at the time of death. Generally, assets are included in the gross estate at their fair market value at the date of death but the executor may elect an alternative valuation date.

Guardian. There are two classes of guardians: (1) A guardian of the person is appointed by the surviving spouse in his or her will to take care of the personal affairs of the couple's minor children. Since each parent is the natural guardian of the minor children, only the surviving parent can name the guardian of the person. (2) A guardian of the property of a minor or incompetent is a person or institution appointed or named to represent the interests of a minor child or incompetent adult. A guardian of the property can be named in a will or be appointed by a court.

Guardian ad litem. A lawyer or other qualified individual appointed by the court to represent the interests of minors or incompetents in a particular matter before the court.

Health Care Proxy. An individual may execute a health care proxy in which he/she sets forth his/her decisions with respect to receiving or refusing medical care and interventions and names the proxy who is to communicate those decisions at the relevant time. In addition, the health care proxy can name an agent authorized to make medical-related decisions on behalf of the principal. The document can be a combination— e.g., first, instructing the agent to communicate the written decisions of the principal and, second, instructing the agent to make decisions in the patient's best interests where instructions relevant to a particular issue are not contained in the document. By no means is a proxy that merely names a person to make all decisions for the principal a good substitute for carefully drafting a personal health care decisions declaration ("living will") tailored to the principal's wishes, needs, and quality of life standards.

Heir. A person designated by law to succeed to the estate of a person who dies intestate (without a will).

Holographic will. A will entirely in the handwriting of the testator. In many states, such a will is not recognized unless it is published, declared, and witnessed as required by statute for other written wills.

Incompetent. An individual who legally has been found incapable of managing his or her own affairs.

Inheritance tax. A tax levied on the rights of the heirs to receive property from a deceased person, measured by the share passing to each beneficiary (sometimes called a succession tax). The Federal death tax is an estate (as opposed to an inheritance) tax. Some states have estate taxes but most have inheritance taxes.

Insurance trust. A trust composed partly or wholly of life insurance policy contracts. An insurance trust is generally established to purchase (or receive as a gift) one or more life insurance policies so that the trust, rather than the insured person, is the owner of the policy. Since the insured person is not the owner, when he or she dies, the value of the policy will not be included in his or her taxable estate. The trust will also be named as the beneficiary of the policies. The trustee can use the policy proceeds to purchase illiquid assets from the insured person's estate, thereby providing liquidity to the estate. If preferred, the trustee could also be authorized to make loans to the estate.

Intangible property. Property that does not have physical substance. The item itself is only the evidence of value (for example, a certificate of stock or bond, an insurance policy, copyright and other intellectual property rights).

Inter vivos trust. A trust created during the grantor's lifetime and operative during lifetime, as opposed to a trust under a will, called a testamentary trust, which does not go into effect until after the grantor dies.

Intestacy laws. Individual state laws that provide for distribution of property of a person who has died without leaving a valid will. Intestate — without a will. A person who dies without a valid will dies intestate.

Inventory. When used as a legal term refers to a schedule of all the assets of an estate, to be prepared by the personal representative (executor). Inventory is also used to refer specifically to creating a record of the artistic output of the artist. A complete inventory and documentation of the artist's work is called a *catalogue raisonné*.

Irrevocable trust. A trust that cannot be revoked or terminated by the grantor. To qualify the trust as irrevocable for tax purposes, the grantor cannot retain any right to alter, amend, revoke, or terminate. The trust can be revoked or terminated by the grantor only with the consent of someone who has an adverse interest in the trust.

Issue. All persons descending from a common ancestor.

Joint tenancy. A common ownership of property by two persons in such a way that, on the death of either, the property goes to the survivor. Under the law of some states, if the persons are husband and wife, then the property is said to be held by the entireties. This is contrasted to tenancy in common, in which each owner has an undivided interest that upon the death of one is passed by probate or intestacy.

Lapse. The failure of a testamentary bequest due to the death of the recipient during the life of the person who made the will.

Legacy. Technically, a gift of personal property by will, but in practice including any disposition by will.

Legatee. A person to whom a legacy is bequeathed under a will.

Life estate. The title of the interest owned by a life tenant; a person whose interest in property terminates at his or her death. "I give my loft to my companion Dario for his life, then to the _____."

Life insurance. An insurance policy payable on the death of the insured person. If an artist wishes to avoid the sale of all work from the artist's estate to pay debts and administrative expenses, the artist may wish to consider life insurance so that the proceeds from the life insurance policy may be used to pay obligations. The designated beneficiary may be the artists' estate or the trustee named in the artist's will if a testamentary trust is created. While providing for liquidity, there may be adverse estate tax consequences to this strategy.

Literary executor. A term sometimes used in the will of an author to authorize a person to assemble unpublished works of the deceased and to try to have published those works the literary executor thinks appropriate, discarding the remainder. In New York, there is no statutory provision for a literary or an art executor. It is possible to designate different executors for different purposes including art and finances.

Living will. A written expression of an individual's desire that no extraordinary means be employed to prolong his or her life. Living wills are legal in some states. In other states, although the living will itself has no legal effect, it can help physicians by making them aware of a patient's wishes.

Marital deduction. For Federal estate tax purposes, the portion of a decedent's estate that may be passed to the surviving spouse without its becoming subject to the Federal estate tax levied against the decedent's estate. Under present Federal estate-tax law, the marital deduction is unlimited, provided that the property passes to the surviving spouse in a qualified manner.

Minor. A person who is under the legal age of majority, which can vary from age 18 to 21, depending on the state law.

Mutual wills. The separate wills of two or more persons, with reciprocal provisions in each will in favor of the other person(s).

Nonliquid assets. Assets that are not readily convertible into cash for at least nine months without a serious loss (such as art, real estate, property, contract rights, and business interests).

Nonprobate property or assets. Property that passes outside the administration of the estate other than by will or intestacy laws. Their distribution is controlled by contract or by operation of law. Examples include jointly held property, pension, benefits and life insurance proceeds paid to a named beneficiary, or property in an inter vivos trust. Nonprobate assets are still included in the gross estate for estate tax purposes.

Nuncupative will. An oral will, declared by the testator in his or her last illness before a sufficient number of witnesses, and afterward reduced to writing.

Ordinary income property. Ordinary income property is treated differently from capital gain property for Federal income tax purposes. Property is ordinary income property if it was created by the donor; it was received by the donor as a gift from the creator; it is held in inventory by a dealer; it would produce short-term capital gain if sold, that is, it is owned for one year or less before being contributed; or it would produce a capital loss if sold. All works of art created by the artist will be ordinary income property, since that property, by the definition contained in the Code, cannot be a capital asset. Artist Jackson Krasner gives his admirer, Lisa Guggenheim, an original painting. The painting retains its character as ordinary income property.

Per capita. Equally to each individual. In distribution per capita, the takers share equally without a right of representation. For example, each of five sons would take one-fifth of the estate. In most states, if descendants are related in equal degree to the decedent, they take per capita; if descendants are of unequal degree (such as four sons and a child of a deceased son), a per stirpes distribution is made.

Per stirpes. "By stock." A distribution per stirpes occurs when issue succeed to the shares of their lineal ascendants by representation. For example, if a person dies survived by three children and by two children of a deceased child (the decedent's grandchildren), distribution is per stirpes. The two grandchildren succeed to their deceased parent's share, so that one-quarter of the estate goes to each of the surviving children, and one-eighth to each of the two grandchildren.

Pourover. The transfer of property from an estate or trust to another estate or trust upon the occurrence of an event specified in the instrument. For example, a will can provide that certain property be paid (poured over) to an existing trust. This is called a pourover will.

Power of appointment. A right given to a person to dispose of property that he or she does not fully own. There are two types of powers of appointment. A general power of appointment is a power over the distribution of property exercisable in favor of any person the donee of the power may select—including himself, his estate, his creditors, or the creditors of his estate. A limited power of appointment is sometimes called a special power. An example of a limited power is giving the recipient of a power the right to distribute the property at her death to any of her sister's children that she designates. Powers of appointment can be created to be exercisable during the power holder's life or can be testamentary powers exercisable by the power holder's will.

Power of attorney. A written document that enables an individual, or "principal," to designate another person or persons as his or her "attorney in fact"—that is, to act on the principal's behalf. The scope of the power can be severely limited or quite broad. (A "durable power" is one that survives the mental or physical incapacity of the creator of the power.)

Present interest. A present right to use or enjoy property or an interest which is presently ascertainable but may vest in the future. Only a gift of an ascertainable present interest is eligible for a charitable deduction. "I give my 'Self Portrait 1992' to my daughter for ten years, then to the M museum." The M museum has a present interest.

Pretermitted heir. A child or other descendant omitted from a testator's will. When a testator fails to make provisions for a child, either living at execution of the will or born thereafter, statutes often provide that such child, or the issue of a deceased child, take an intestate share of the testator's estate.

Principal. The property comprising the estate or fund that has been set aside in trust, or from which income has been expected to accrue. The trust principal is also known as the trust corpus or res.

Probate. The process of proving the validity of the will and executing its provisions under the guidance of the appropriate public official. The title of the official varies from state to state. Wills are probated in the Register of Wills office and in the Probate or Surrogate's Court. When a person dies, the will must be filed before the proper officer; this is called filing or offering the will for probate. When it has been filed and accepted, it is said to be admitted to probate. The process of probating the will involves recognition by the court of the executor named in the will (or appointment of an administrator if none has been named).

Probate property. Property that can be passed under the terms of the will or (if no will) under the intestacy laws of the state.

Prudent man rule (or Prudent investor law). The theory according to which the duty of an executor is to invest in such assets as an ordinary, prudent man of intelligence and integrity would purchase in the exercise of reasonable care, judgment, and diligence under the circumstances existing at the time of purchase.

Qualified appraisal. An appraisal prepared by a qualified appraiser not earlier than sixty days before the date of the contribution of the appraised property. The appraisal must be signed and dated by a qualified appraiser who charges an appraisal fee that is not based on a percentage of value and that contains certain required information set forth in Treas. Req. Section 1.170A-13(b)(2)(ii).

1. A description of the property in sufficient detail for a person who is not generally familiar with the type of property to determine that the property appraised is the property that was (or will be) contributed.

2. The physical condition of any tangible property.

3. The date (or expected date) of contribution.

4. The terms of any agreement or understanding entered into (or expected to be entered into) by or on behalf of the donor that relates to the use, sale, or other disposition of the donated property.

5. The name, address, and taxpayer identification number of the qualified appraiser and, if the appraiser is a partner, an employee, or an independent contractor engaged by a person other than the donor, the name, address, and taxpayer identification number of the partnership or the person who employs or engages the appraiser.

6. The qualifications of the qualified appraiser who signs the appraisal, including the appraiser's background, experience, education, and any membership in professional appraisal associations.

7. A statement that the appraisal was prepared for income tax purposes.

8. The date (or dates) on which the property was valued.

9. The appraised FMV on the date (or expected date) of contribution.

10. The method of valuation used to determine FMV, such as the income approach, the comparable sales or market data approach, or the replacement cost less depreciation approach, and

11. The specific basis for the valuation, such as any specific comparable sales transaction.

Qualified Appraiser. A person who holds himself or herself out to the public as an appraiser who is an expert as to the particular type of property being appraised; who understands that, if he or she makes a false or fraudulent overstatement of value, he or she may be subject to a civil penalty under Section 6701; and who is completely independent of the donor. To be independent of the donor, the qualified appraiser cannot be the donor or the donee, a party to the transaction in which the donor acquired the property, a person employed by any of the foregoing, or a person related (within the meaning of Section 267(b)) to any of the foregoing.

Receipt and release. Informal method of settling estates. The executor gives the beneficiaries an informal accounting and obtains a "receipt" from the beneficiaries for their share of the estate and a "release" discharging the executor from any further liability.

Remainderman. The person(s) or entity(ies) entitled to receive property (usually in trust) after the termination of the prior holder's interest. For example, a mother might set up a trust that pays her income for life, but at her death the principal in the trust would pass to her son (the remainderman).

Renunciation. Also called a disclaimer. An unqualified refusal to accept property or an interest in property. It is the abandonment of a right without the direct transfer to someone else of the interest subject to that right. The renounced or disclaimed property passes as though the person renouncing/disclaiming the property has died before the property was transferred to him or her.

Residuary estate. The remaining part of the decedent's estate after payment of debts and bequests. Wills usually contain a clause disposing of the residue of the estate that the decedent has not otherwise bequeathed or devised.

Reversionary interest. A right to future enjoyment by the transferor of property that is now in the possession or enjoyment of another party. For example, a father creates a trust under which his son is going to enjoy the income for life, with the principal of the trust to be paid over to the daughter at the son's death or, if the daughter does not survive the son, the remainder will revert to the father. The father's interest is the reversionary interest.

Revocable trust. A trust that can be changed or terminated during the grantor's lifetime and under which the property in the trust can be recovered. West Coast lawyers think its the hottest thing going. East Coast lawyers tend to be slightly less enthusiastic, as one prominent trust and estate's practitioner commented, "One of the great myths is that the revocable trust completely avoids probate. 99.9 per cent of the time it does not. It is particularly difficult to transfer all your artwork to a trust."

State Death Tax Equal to Federal Credit (SOP Tax). A death tax imposed by a state equal to the amount of the Federal estate tax credited for state death taxes paid.

Tenant in common. Tenants who hold an undivided interest in the same property without right of survivorship. Each tenant has the right to bequeath, sell, or give her undivided share. For example, if artist gifts an undivided one-half interest in a sculpture created by her to the Hirschorn Museum, the artist and Hirschorn are tenants in common. "I hereby grant to the Hirschorn Museum an undivided one-half interest in my sculpture. The museum shall have the right to possession and control for six months a year."

Trust. An express trust of property created by a will, deed, or other instrument, whereby there is imposed upon a trustee the duty to administer property for the benefit of a named or other described individual.

The trustee is the legal owner of the trust property and the beneficiary is the beneficial owner. The document which creates the trust must define what property is to be transferred to the trust, i.e., how and to what extent the trust is to be funded. "I give, devise, and bequeath to the Norman Rockwell Art Collection Trust established under a Trust agreement dated October 25, 1973, by and between myself as Settlor and ... Thomas Rockwell as Trustee, the building which I have used as my studio together with the contents thereof at the time of my death, including but not limited to any works of art done by me or others, to be held and administered in accordance with the terms and conditions, thereof."

Trustee. The person holding legal title to a trust for the benefit of a beneficiary. As legal owner, the trustee controls the management, disposition, etc., of the trust property.

Vested interest. A present right or title to a thing which carries with it an existing right of alienation (sale or gift or devise) even though the right to possession or enjoyment may be postponed to some uncertain time in the future. Distinguished from a future interest which may never materialize or ripen into title. It is the right to entitlement or possession that distinguishes a vested present interest from a future interest. Freda Kahlo by deed of gift transfers to the Diego Rivera Museum an undivided quarter interest in "Self Portrait." One year later she transfers by deed of gift, a three-quarters interest in "Self Portrait" to take effect on her death to the National Museum of Women's Art. The National Museum has a vested present interest in the painting. Only a present vested interest to a charity is eligible for a charitable deduction.

Will. The legal expression or declaration of a person's mind or wishes as to the disposition of her or his property to be performed or take effect at death. Formal requirements vary by states, but usually, at a minimum, a will must be in writing made with testamentary intent and mental capacity, and signed by the testator. Requirements for witnesses vary according to states. New York's Estate, Powers and Trust Law does not refer to a prescribed format for a will but does prescribe formalities for execution and witnessing of the will. When Georgia O'Keeffe, died in 1986 at age 98, the principal beneficiary of her will was Juan Hamilton, who was 58 years her junior. An aspiring but nearly destitute artist, Hamilton had knocked on O'Keeffe's door one morning in August of 1973 seeking work. He never left. O'Keeffe initially employed Hamilton as her secretary, but he ultimately became her assistant, agent, business manager, companion, and caretaker. After O'Keeffe's death, her 92-year-old sister and a niece challenged the validity of O'Keeffe's will, claiming Hamilton exercised undue influence over her.

A Visual Artist's Guide to Estate Planning

Appendices

APPENDIX A:

Inventory Worksheets

SAMPLE INVENTORY/CATALOG WORKSHEET

REF#:

TITLE:

DATE:

MEDIUM:

SIZE:

SIGNATURE:

INSCRIPTION:

GALLERY REF:

PUBLICATIONS:

EXHIBITIONS: (SPACE FOR IMAGE)

INFORMATION FOR CREATING AN INVENTORY/CATALOG WORKSHEET

The simplest method is to start with a lined-paper notebook and to add vertical lines to provide columns, headed as shown below. This allows the use of a single line per entry.

Example:

NUMBER	TITLE	DATE	MEDIUM	SIZE	LOCATION
#10001	"Untitled"	1987	oil on canvas	70 x 80	studio closet
#10002	"Untitled"	1995	wood & metal	44 x 90 x 10	studio wall
#10003	"John Doe"	1967	pencil on paper	9 x 5	folder #3

The most effective approach for making an initial inventory is to simply start at one location (building, floor, room, closet, etc.) and list every item found before moving on to the next

COMMENTS

1. Number:

It is essential to assign a set of sequential numbers and wherever possible to tag or mark each place or its container. Since it is not unusual for some descriptions as to title, medium, size, etc., to be virtually identical, the assigned number often simplifies or enables identification. The same numbers should be used to identify photographs and other documentation relating to each place.

2. Title:

It is best to use quotation marks to distinguish an actual title from the same words used as comments or descriptions (e.g., untitled, composition). This is also the best place to note if a piece is unfinished or a "study" for something else.

3. Date:

Even if the actual date is unknown, it is useful to indicate a range or guess

(e.g., c.1968, 1978?).

4. Medium:

Generalizations (painting, drawing, etc.) should be avoided in favor of specifics such as "oil on canvas." Modern synthetics or unusual mediums should include brand names.

5. Size:

It is now standard to list height x width x depth, but it is clearer if that is shown in the column heading or noted at the beginning of the list. Differences, such as between image and sheet sizes, should be noted.

6. Location:

This should be as specific as possible and should be kept current by noting changes. It is helpful to add a "SHIPMENT" or "IN/OUT" column to indicate both temporary changes such as loans, and permanent changes such as sales and gifts.

7. Signature:

It is important to record if and where each work is signed, whether in a separate column or in the "TITLE" field.

Please note that off-the-shelf inventory programs for personal computers are now widely available or can be easily devised. Whether hand-written or computerized, an inventory can be the first step toward organizing other documentation such as exhibition and publication histories.

APPENDIX B:

Copyright Office Form VA and Related Materials:

In Answer to Your Query

IN ANSWER TO YOUR QUERY

COPYRIGHT REGISTRATION OF VISUAL ARTS

LIBRARY
OF
CONGRESS

Washington
D.C.
20559-6000

The visual arts category consists of pictorial, graphic, or sculptural works, including 2-dimensional and 3-dimensional works of fine, graphic, and applied art, photographs, prints and art reproductions, maps, globes, charts, technical drawings, diagrams, architectural works and models.

Copyright protects an author's specific expression in literary, artistic, or musical form. Copyright protection does not extend to any idea, system, method, device, name or title.

To register a work of the visual arts, send the following three elements **in the same envelope or package** to the Register of Copyrights, Copyright Office, Library of Congress, Washington, D.C. 20559-6000:

   1. A completed application Form VA.

   2. A nonrefundable filing fee of $20.00.*

   3. A nonreturnable deposit of the material to be registered. The deposit requirements will vary depending on the nature of the work and whether the work has been published prior to registration.

If the visual art is *published*, the proper deposit is, generally, two complete copies. Identifying material may be deposited in some cases. If the visual art is *unpublished*, generally one complete copy is required. This copy must represent the entire copyrightable content of the work for which registration is sought.

Identifying material deposited to represent the visual art shall usually consist of photographs, photostats, slides, drawings, or other 2-dimensional representations of the work. The identifying material shall include as many pieces as necessary to show the entire copyrightable content of the work, including any copyright notice on the work. All pieces of identifying material other than transparencies must be no less than 3 x 3 inches in size, and not more than 9 x 12 inches, but preferably 8 x 10 inches. At least one piece of identifying material must, on its front, back, or mount, indicate the title of the work and an exact measurement of one or more dimensions of the work. (See Circular 40a, Deposit Requirements for Registration of Claims to Copyright in Visual Arts Material and Circular 40, Copyright Registration for Works of the Visual Arts.)

Sincerely yours,

Register of Copyrights

*The fees for registration of copyright claims, recordation of documents, recordation of NIEs, certifications, searches, filing notice of intention to make and distribute phonorecords, and receipt for deposits are effective through June 30, **1999**. For more information, please write the Copyright Office, check the Copyright Office Website at http://www.loc.gov/copyright, or call (202) 707-3000 for the latest fee information.

Enclosures

Copyright Registration
of Visual Arts
September 1996—75,000

How Long Does Copyright Registration Take?

A copyright registration is effective on the date of receipt in the Copyright Office of all required elements in acceptable form, regardless of the length of time it takes to process the application and mail the certificate of registration. The length of time required by the Copyright Office to process an application varies from time to time, depending on the amount of material received and the personnel available to handle it. It must also be kept in mind that it takes a number of days for mail to reach the Copyright Office and for the certificate of registration to reach the recipient after being mailed from the Copyright Office.

You will receive no acknowledgement that your application for copyright registration has been received (the Office receives more than 500,000 applications annually), but you may expect:

- A letter or telephone call from a Copyright Office staff member if further information is needed; and
- A certificate of registration to indicate the work has been registered, or if the application cannot be accepted, a letter explaining why it has been rejected.

You might not receive either of these until at least 120 days have passed.

If you want to know when the Copyright Office received your material, you should send it via registered or certified mail and request a return receipt.

For further information, write:
Information Section, LM-401
Copyright Office
Library of Congress
Washington, D.C. 20559-6000

If you need additional application forms for copyright registration, call (202) 707-9100, at any time. Leave your request as a recorded message on the Copyright Office Forms Hotline in Washington, D.C.; please specify the kind and number of forms you need. If you have general information questions and wish to talk to an information specialist, call (202) 707-3000, TTY (202) 707-6737.

You may also photocopy blank application forms; **however,** photocopied forms submitted to the Copyright Office must be clear, legible, on a good grade of 8½-inch by 11-inch white paper, suitable for automatic feeding through a photocopier. The forms should be printed, preferably in black ink, head-to-head (so that when you turn the sheet over, the top of page 2 is directly behind the top of page 1). **Forms not meeting these requirements will be returned to the originator.**

All U.S. Copyright Office application forms are now available on the Internet. They may be downloaded and printed for use in registering a claim to copyright or for use in renewing a claim to copyright.

The forms and the format may be accessed and downloaded by connecting to the Library of Congress home page on the World Wide Web (WWW) and selecting the copyright link.

The address is:
http://www.loc.gov

Or you may connect through the Copyright Office home page.

The address is:
http://www.loc.gov/copyright

You must have Adobe® Acrobat® Reader installed on your computer to view and print the forms. The free Adobe® Acrobat® Reader may be downloaded from Adobe Systems Incorporated through links from the same Internet site at which the forms are available.

Print forms head to head (top of page 2 is directly behind the top of page 1) on a single piece of good quality, 8½-inch by 11-inch white paper. To achieve the best quality copies of the application forms, use a laser printer.

Frequently requested Copyright Office circulars, announcements, and recently proposed as well as final regulations are also available over the Internet.

Copyright Office circulars and announcements are available via fax. Call **(202) 707-2600** from any touchtone telephone. Key in your fax number at the prompt and the document number of the item(s) you want to receive by fax. The item(s) will be transmitted to your fax machine. If you do not know the document number of the item(s) you want, you may request that a menu be faxed to you. You may order up to three items at a time. Note that copyright application forms are *not* available by fax.

You might not receive either of these until approximately 6 months after submission (8 months in the case of Visual Arts claims).

APPENDIX C:

Form VA

FORM VA
For a Work of the Visual Arts
UNITED STATES COPYRIGHT OFFICE

REGISTRATION NUMBER

_____

VA   VAU

EFFECTIVE DATE OF REGISTRATION

_____

Month   Day   Year

DO NOT WRITE ABOVE THIS LINE. IF YOU NEED MORE SPACE, USE A SEPARATE CONTINUATION SHEET.

1 **TITLE OF THIS WORK** ▼

NATURE OF THIS WORK ▼ See instructions

PREVIOUS OR ALTERNATIVE TITLES ▼

PUBLICATION AS A CONTRIBUTION If this work was published as a contribution to a periodical, serial, or collection, give information about the collective work in which the contribution appeared.   **Title of Collective Work** ▼

If published in a periodical or serial give: **Volume** ▼   **Number** ▼   **Issue Date** ▼   **On Pages** ▼

---

2 **a** **NAME OF AUTHOR** ▼

DATES OF BIRTH AND DEATH
Year Born ▼   Year Died ▼

Was this contribution to the work a
"work made for hire"?
☐ Yes
☐ No

AUTHOR'S NATIONALITY OR DOMICILE
Name of Country

OR { Citizen of ▶ _____
     Domiciled in ▶ _____

**WAS THIS AUTHOR'S CONTRIBUTION TO
THE WORK**
Anonymous?   ☐ Yes   ☐ No
Pseudonymous?   ☐ Yes   ☐ No

If the answer to either
of these questions is
"Yes," see detailed
instructions.

NOTE

Under the law, the "author" of a "work made for hire" is generally the employer, not the employee (see instructions). For any part of this work that was "made for hire" check "Yes" in the space provided, give the employer (or other person for whom the work was prepared) as "Author" of that part, and leave the space for dates of birth and death blank.

NATURE OF AUTHORSHIP Check appropriate box(es). **See instructions**

☐ 3-Dimensional sculpture ☐ Map ☐ Technical drawing
☐ 2-Dimensional artwork ☐ Photograph ☐ Text
☐ Reproduction of work of art ☐ Jewelry design ☐ Architectural work
☐ Design on sheetlike material

NAME OF AUTHOR ▼

DATES OF BIRTH AND DEATH
Year Born ▼   Year Died ▼

Was this contribution to the work a "work made for hire"?
☐ Yes
☐ No

AUTHOR'S NATIONALITY OR DOMICILE
Name of Country
OR ⎨ Citizen of ▶
     ⎩ Domiciled in ▶

WAS THIS AUTHOR'S CONTRIBUTION TO THE WORK
Anonymous? ☐ Yes ☐ No
Pseudonymous? ☐ Yes ☐ No

If the answer to either of these questions is "Yes," see detailed instructions.

NATURE OF AUTHORSHIP Check appropriate box(es). **See instructions**

☐ 3-Dimensional sculpture ☐ Map ☐ Technical drawing
☐ 2-Dimensional artwork ☐ Photograph ☐ Text
☐ Reproduction of work of art ☐ Jewelry design ☐ Architectural work
☐ Design on sheetlike material

3

a YEAR IN WHICH CREATION OF THIS WORK WAS COMPLETED This information must be given ▼ Year in all cases.

b DATE AND NATION OF FIRST PUBLICATION OF THIS PARTICULAR WORK
Complete this information Month ▶   Day ▶   Year ▶
ONLY if this work
has been published.   ◀ Nation

4

See instructions before completing this space.

COPYRIGHT CLAIMANT(S) Name and address must be given even if the claimant is the same as the author given in space 2. ▼

TRANSFER If the claimant(s) named here in space 4 is (are) different from the author(s) named in space 2, give a brief statement of how the claimant(s) obtained ownership of the copyright. ▼

DO NOT WRITE HERE
OFFICE USE ONLY

APPLICATION RECEIVED

ONE DEPOSIT RECEIVED

TWO DEPOSITS RECEIVED

FUNDS RECEIVED

MORE ON BACK ▶ • Complete all applicable spaces (numbers 5-9) on the reverse side of this page.
                    • See detailed instructions.   • Sign the form at line 8.

EXAMINED BY

CHECKED BY

CORRESPONDENCE
☐ Yes

FOR
COPYRIGHT
OFFICE
USE
ONLY

FORM VA

DO NOT WRITE ABOVE THIS LINE. IF YOU NEED MORE SPACE, USE A SEPARATE CONTINUATION SHEET.

PREVIOUS REGISTRATION Has registration for this work, or for an earlier version of this work, already been made in the Copyright Office?

☐ **Yes** ☐ **No** If your answer is "Yes," why is another registration being sought? (Check appropriate box.) ▼

a. ☐ This is the first published edition of a work previously registered in unpublished form.

b. ☐ This is the first application submitted by this author as copyright claimant.

c. ☐ This is a changed version of the work, as shown by space 6 on this application.

If your answer is "Yes," give: **Previous Registration Number** ▼   **Year of Registration** ▼

5

DERIVATIVE WORK OR COMPILATION Complete both space 6a and 6b for a derivative work; complete only 6b for a compilation.

a. **Preexisting Material** Identify any preexisting work or works that this work is based on or incorporates. ▼

b. **Material Added to This Work** Give a brief, general statement of the material that has been added to this work and in which copyright is claimed. ▼

6

a

See instructions
before completing
this space.

b

DEPOSIT ACCOUNT If the registration fee is to be charged to a Deposit Account established in the Copyright Office, give name and number of Account.

Name ▼   **Account Number** ▼

7

a

CORRESPONDENCE Give name and address to which correspondence about this application should be sent. Name/Address/Apt/City/State/ZIP ▼

b

Area code and daytime telephone number ▼   Fax number ▶

CERTIFICATION* I, the undersigned, hereby certify that I am the

8

check only one ▶

☐ author
☐ other copyright claimant
☐ owner of exclusive right(s)
☐ authorized agent of _____
Name of author or other copyright claimant, or owner of exclusive right(s) ▲

of the work identified in this application and that the statements made
by me in this application are correct to the best of my knowledge.

Typed or printed name and date ▼ If this application gives a date of publication in space 3, do not sign and submit it before that date.

_____   Date▶ _____

Handwritten signature (X) ▼

Mail
certificate
to:

Certificate
will be
mailed in
window
envelope

Name ▼

Number/Street/Apt ▼

City/State/ZIP ▼

9

YOU MUST:
• Complete all necessary spaces
• Sign your application in space 8

SEND ALL 3 ELEMENTS
IN THE SAME PACKAGE:
1. Application form
2. Nonrefundable $20 filing fee
   in check or money order
   payable to *Register of Copyrights*
3. Deposit material

MAIL TO:
Register of Copyrights, Library of Congress
101 Independence Ave., S.E.
Washington, D.C. 20559-6000

April 1997—300,000   ♻ PRINTED ON RECYCLED PAPER   ☆U.S. GOVERNMENT PRINTING OFFICE: 1997–417-750/40,036

APPENDIX D:

Filling Out Application Form VA

Application Form VA

Detach and read these instructions before completing this form.
Make sure all applicable spaces have been filled in before you return this form.

BASIC INFORMATION

When to Use This Form: Use Form VA for copyright registration of published or unpublished works of the visual arts. This category consists of "pictorial, graphic, or sculptural works," including two-dimensional and three-dimensional works of fine, graphic, and applied art, photographs, prints and art reproductions, maps, globes, charts, technical drawings, diagrams, and models.

To make registration easier, you may use Short Form VA if you are not an anonymous author; you are the only author and copyright owner of the work; the work is not made for hire; and the work is completely new without a substantial amount of material in the public domain or material that was previously published or registered.

What Does Copyright Protect? Copyright in a work of the visual arts protects those pictorial, graphic, or sculptural elements that, either alone or in combination, represent an "original work of authorship." The statute declares: "In no case does copyright protection for an original work of authorship extend to any idea, procedure, process, system, method of operation, concept, principle, or discovery, regardless of the form in which it is described, explained, illustrated, or embodied in such work."

Works of Artistic Craftsmanship and Designs: "Works of artistic craftsmanship" are registrable on Form VA, but the statute makes clear that protection extends to "their form" and not to "their mechanical or utilitarian aspects." The "design of a useful article" is considered copyrightable "only if, and only to the extent that, such design incorporates pictorial, graphic, or sculptural features that can be identified separately from, and are capable of existing independently of, the utilitarian aspects of the article."

Labels and Advertisements: Works prepared for use in connection with the sale or advertisement of goods and services are registrable if they contain "original work of authorship." Use Form VA if the copyrightable material in the work you are registering is mainly pictorial or graphic; use Form TX if it consists mainly of text. **NOTE:** Words and short phrases such as names, titles, and slogans cannot be protected by copyright, and the same is true of standard symbols, emblems, and other commonly used graphic designs that are in the public domain. When used commercially, material of that sort can sometimes be protected under state laws of unfair competition or under the Federal trademark laws. For information about trademark registration, write to the Commissioner of Patents and Trademarks, Washington, D.C. 20231.

Architectural Works: Copyright protection extends to the design of buildings created for the use of human beings. Architectural works created on or after December 1, 1990, or that on December 1, 1990, were unconstructed and embodied only in unpublished plans or drawings are eligible. Request Circular 41 for more information. Architectural works and technical drawings cannot be registered on the same application.

Deposit to Accompany Application: An application for copyright registration must be accompanied by a deposit consisting of copies representing the entire work for which registration is to be made.

Unpublished Work: Deposit one complete copy.
Published Work: Deposit two complete copies of the best edition.
Work First Published Outside the United States: Deposit one complete copy of the first foreign edition.
Contribution to a Collective Work: Deposit one complete copy of the best edition of the collective work.

The Copyright Notice: For works first published on or after March 1, 1989, the law provides that a copyright notice in a specified form "may be placed on all publicly distributed copies from which the work can be visually perceived." Use of the copyright notice is the responsibility of the copyright owner and does not require permission from the Copyright Office. The notice for visually perceptible copies should contain the following three elements: (1) the symbol "©", or the word "Copyright," or the abbreviation "Copr."; (2) the year of first publication; and (3) the name of the owner of copyright. For example: "© 1997 Jane Cole." The notice should be affixed to the copies "in such manner and location as to give reasonable notice of the claim of copyright." Notice was required to be placed on each published copy of a work under the 1976 Copyright Act as originally enacted. Failure to do so could result in the loss of copyright protection. The notice requirement was eliminated when the United States adhered to the Berne Convention effective March 1, 1989. As of 1996, the Uruguay Round Agreements Act restored copyright in certain foreign works that entered the public domain in the United States because they were originally published without notice.

For information about notice requirements for works published before March 1, 1989, or other copyright information, write: Publication Section, LM-455, Library of Congress, Copyright Office, 101 Independence Ave., S.E., Washington, D.C. 20559-6000.

SPACE 1: Title

Title of This Work: Every work submitted for copyright registration must be given a title to identify that particular work. If the copies of the work bear a title (or an identifying phrase that could serve as a title), transcribe that wording *completely* and *exactly* on the application. Indexing of the registration and future identification of the work will depend on the information you give here. For an architectural work that has been constructed, add the date of construction after the title; if unconstructed at this time, add "not yet constructed."

Publication as a Contribution: If the work being registered is a contribution to a periodical, serial, or collection, give the title of the contribution in the "Title of This Work" space. Then, in the line headed "Publication as a Contribution," give information about the collective work in which the contribution appeared.

Nature of This Work: Briefly describe the general nature or character of the pictorial, graphic, or sculptural work being registered for copyright. Examples: "Oil Painting"; "Charcoal Drawing"; "Etching"; "Sculpture"; "Map"; "Photograph"; "Scale Model"; "Lithographic Print"; "Jewelry Design"; "Fabric Design."

Previous or Alternative Titles: Complete this space if there are any additional titles for the work under which someone searching for the registration might be likely to look, or under which a document pertaining to the work might be recorded.

SPACE 2: Author(s)

General Instruction: After reading these instructions, decide who are the "authors" of this work for copyright purposes. Then, unless the work is a "collective work," give the requested information about every "author" who contributed any appreciable amount of copyrightable matter to this version of the work. If you need further space, request Continuation Sheets. In the case of a collective work, such as a catalog of paintings or collection of cartoons by various authors, give information about the author of the collective work as a whole.

Name of Author: The fullest form of the author's name should be given. Unless the work was "made for hire," the individual who actually created the work is its "author." In the case of a work made for hire, the statute provides that "the employer or other person for whom the work was prepared is considered the author."

What is a "Work Made for Hire"? A "work made for hire" is defined as: (1) "a work prepared by an employee within the scope of his or her employment"; or (2) "a work specially ordered or commissioned for use as a contribution to a collective work, as a part of a motion picture or other audiovisual work, as a translation, as a supplementary work, as a compilation, as an instructional text, as a test, as answer material for a test, or as an atlas, if the parties expressly agree in a written instrument signed by them that the work shall be considered a work made for hire." If you have checked "Yes" to indicate that the work was "made for hire," you must give the full legal name of the employer (or other person for whom the work was prepared). You may also include the name of the employee along with the name of the employer (for example: "Elster Publishing Co., employer for hire of John Ferguson").

"Anonymous" or "Pseudonymous" Work: An author's contribution to a work is "anonymous" if that author is not identified on the copies or phonorecords of the work. An author's contribution to a work is "pseudonymous" if that author is identified on the copies or phonorecords under a fictitious name. If the work is "anonymous" you may: (1) leave the line blank; or (2) state "anonymous" on the line; or (3) reveal the author's identity. If the work is "pseudonymous" you may: (1) leave the line blank; or (2) give the pseudonym and identify it as such (for example: "Huntley Haverstock, pseudonym"); or (3) reveal the author's name, making clear which is the real name and which is the pseudonym (for example: "Henry Leek, whose pseudonym is Priam Farrel"). However, the citizenship or domicile of the author **must be given in all cases.**

Dates of Birth and Death: If the author is dead, the statute requires that the year of death be included in the application unless the work is anonymous or pseudonymous. The author's birth date is optional but is useful as a form of identification. Leave this space blank if the author's contribution was a "work made for hire."

Author's Nationality or Domicile: Give the country of which the author is a citizen or the country in which the author is domiciled. Nationality or domicile **must** be given in all cases.

Nature of Authorship: Categories of pictorial, graphic, and sculptural authorship are listed below. Check the box(es) that best describe(s) each author's contribution to the work.

3-Dimensional sculptures: fine art sculptures, toys, dolls, scale models, and sculptural designs applied to useful articles.

2-Dimensional artwork: watercolor and oil paintings; pen and ink drawings; logo illustrations; greeting cards; collages; stencils; patterns; computer graphics; graphics appearing in screen displays; artwork appearing on posters, calendars, games, commercial prints and labels, and packaging, as well as 2-dimensional artwork applied to useful articles, and designs reproduced on textiles, lace, and other fabrics; on wallpaper, carpeting, floor tile, wrapping paper, and clothing.

Reproductions of works of art: reproductions of preexisting artwork made by, for example, lithography, photoengraving, or etching.

Maps: cartographic representations of an area such as state and county maps, atlases, marine charts, relief maps, and globes.

Photographs: pictorial photographic prints and slides and holograms.

Jewelry designs: 3-dimensional designs applied to rings, pendants, earrings, necklaces, and the like.

Designs on sheetlike materials: designs reproduced on textiles, lace, and other fabrics; wallpaper; carpeting; floor tile; wrapping paper; and clothing.

Technical drawings: diagrams illustrating scientific or technical information in linear form such as architectural blueprints or mechanical drawings.

Text: textual material that accompanies pictorial, graphic, or sculptural works such as comic strips, greeting cards, games rules, commercial prints or labels, and maps.

Architectural works: designs of buildings, including the overall form as well as the arrangement and composition of spaces and elements of the design.

NOTE: Any registration for the underlying architectural plans must be applied for on a separate Form VA, checking the box "Technical drawing."

SPACE 5: Previous Registration

General Instructions: The questions in space 5 are intended to find out whether an earlier registration has been made for this work and, if so, whether there is any basis for a new registration. As a rule, only one basic copyright registration can be made for the same version of a particular work.

Same Version: If this version is substantially the same as the work covered by a previous registration, a second registration is not generally possible unless: (1) the work has been registered in unpublished form and a second registration is now being sought to cover this first published edition; or (2) someone other than the author is identified as a copyright claimant in the earlier registration, and the author is now seeking registration in his or her own name. If either of these two exceptions apply, check the appropriate box and give the earlier registration number and date. Otherwise, do not submit Form VA; instead, write the Copyright Office for information about supplementary registration or recordation of transfers of copyright ownership.

Changed Version: If the work has been changed and you are now seeking registration to cover the additions or revisions, check the last box in space 5, give the earlier registration number and date, and complete both parts of space 6 in accordance with the instruction below.

Previous Registration Number and Date: If more than one previous registration has been made for the work, give the number and date of the latest registration.

SPACE 6: Derivative Work or Compilation

General Instructions: Complete space 6 if this work is a "changed version," "compilation," or "derivative work," and if it incorporates one or more earlier works that have already been published or registered for copyright, or that have fallen into the public domain. A "compilation" is defined as "a work formed by the collection and assembling of preexisting materials or of data that are selected, coordinated, or arranged in such a way that the resulting work as a whole constitutes an original work of authorship." A "derivative work" is " a work based on one or more preexisting works."

Examples of derivative works include reproductions of works of art, sculptures based on drawings, lithographs based on paintings, maps based on previously published sources, or "any other form in which a work may be recast, transformed, or adapted." Derivative works also include works "consisting of editorial revisions, annotations, or other modifications" if these changes, as a whole, represent an original work of authorship.

Preexisting Material (space 6a): Complete this space **and** space 6b for derivative works. In this space identify the preexisting work that has been recast, transformed, or adapted. Examples of preexisting material might be "Grunewald Altarpiece" or "19th century quilt design." Do not complete this space for compilations.

Material Added to This Work (space 6b): Give a brief, general statement of the **additional** new material covered by the copyright claim for which registration is sought. In the case of a derivative work, identify this new material. Examples: "Adaptation of design and additional artistic work"; "Reproduction of painting by photolithography"; "Additional cartographic material"; "Compilation of photographs." If the work is a compilation, give a brief, general statement describing both the material that has been compiled **and** the compilation itself. Example: "Compilation of 19th century political cartoons."

SPACE 7,8,9: Fee, Correspondence, Certification, Return Address

Deposit Account: If you maintain a Deposit Account in the Copyright Office, identify it in space 7a. Otherwise leave the space blank and send the fee of $20 with your application and deposit.

Correspondence (space 7b): This space should contain the name, address, area code, and telephone number and fax number (if available) of the person to be consulted if correspondence about this application becomes necessary.

Certification (space 8): The application cannot be accepted unless it bears the date and the **handwritten signature** of the author or other copyright claimant, or of the owner of exclusive right(s), or of the duly authorized agent of the author, claimant, or owner of exclusive right(s).

Address for Return of Certificate (space 9): The address box must be completed legibly since the certificate will be returned in a window envelope.

SPACE 3: Creation and Publication

General Instructions: Do not confuse "creation" with "publication." Every application for copyright registration must state "the year in which creation of the work was completed." Give the date and nation of first publication only if the work has been published.

Creation: Under the statute, a work is "created" when it is fixed in a copy or phonorecord for the first time. Where a work has been prepared over a period of time, the part of the work existing in fixed form on a particular date constitutes the created work on that date. The date you give here should be the year in which the author completed the particular version for which registration is now being sought, even if other versions exist or if further changes or additions are planned.

Publication: The statute defines "publication" as "the distribution of copies or phonorecords of a work to the public by sale or other transfer of ownership, or by rental, lease, or lending"; a work is also "published" if there has been an "offering to distribute copies or phonorecords to a group of persons for purposes of further distribution, public performance, or public display." Give the full date (month, day, year) when, and the country where, publication first occurred. If first publication took place simultaneously in the United States and other countries, it is sufficient to state "U.S.A."

SPACE 4: Claimant(s)

Name(s) and Address(es) of Copyright Claimant(s): Give the name(s) and address(es) of the copyright claimant(s) in this work even if the claimant is the same as the author. Copyright in a work belongs initially to the author of the work (including, in the case of a work made for hire, the employer or other person for whom the work was prepared). The copyright claimant is either the author of the work or a person or organization to whom the copyright initially belonging to the author has been transferred.

Transfer: The statute provides that, if the copyright claimant is not the author, the application for registration must contain "a brief statement of how the claimant obtained ownership of the copyright." If any copyright claimant named in space 4 is not an author named in space 2, give a brief statement explaining how the claimant(s) obtained ownership of the copyright. Examples: "By written contract"; "Transfer of all rights by author"; "Assignment"; "By will." Do not attach transfer documents or other attachments or riders.

APPENDIX E:

Short Form VA

SHORT FORM VA

For a Work of the Visual Arts
UNITED STATES COPYRIGHT OFFICE

REGISTRATION NUMBER

VA   VAU

Effective Date of Registration

Month   Day   Year

Application Received

Deposit Received
One   Two

Fee Received

Examined By

Correspondence ☐

TYPE OR PRINT IN BLACK INK. DO NOT WRITE ABOVE THIS LINE.

1 Title of This Work:

Alternative title or title of larger work
in which this work was published:

**2 Name and Address
of Author/Owner
of the Copyright:**

Nationality or domicile:

Phone and Fax numbers: Phone ( )   Fax ( )

3 Year of Creation:

4 If work has been published, Date and Nation of Publication:

a. Date _____ _____ _____
(Month) (Day) (Year)
(Month, day, and year all required)

b. Nation _____

5 Type of Authorship in This Work:
(Check all that apply.)

☐ 3-Dimensional sculpture ☐ Photograph ☐ Map
☐ 2-Dimensional artwork ☐ Jewelry design ☐ Text
☐ Technical drawing ☐ Architectural work

6 Signature of Author:

I certify that the statements made by me in this application are correct to the best of my knowledge. *

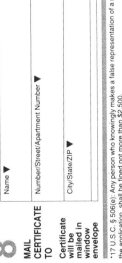

7 Name and Address of Person to Contact for Rights and Permissions: Phone and Fax numbers: E-mail address:

☐ Check here if same as #2 above

Phone ( ) Fax ( )

E-mail

OPTIONAL

8

MAIL CERTIFICATE TO

Certificate will be mailed in window envelope

Name ▼ _____

Number/Street/Apartment Number ▼ _____

City/State/ZIP ▼ _____

9 Deposit Account # _____

Name _____

APPENDIX F:

Instructions for Short Form VA

INSTRUCTIONS FOR SHORT FORM VA

For pictorial, graphic, and sculptural works

USE THIS FORM IF—

1. you are the **only** author and copyright owner of this work; *and*
2. the work was **not** made for hire, *and*
3. the work is completely new (does not contain a substantial amount of material that has been previously published or registered or is in the public domain).

If any of the above does not apply, you must use standard Form VA.
NOTE: Short Form VA is not appropriate for an anonymous author who does not wish to reveal his or her identity.

HOW TO COMPLETE SHORT FORM VA

- Type or print in black ink.
- Be clear and legible. (Your certificate of registration will be copied from your form.)
- Give only the information requested.
- Do **not** use continuation sheets or any other attachments.

1 Title of This Work

You must give a title. If there is no title, state "UNTITLED." If you are registering an unpublished collection, give the collection title you want to appear in our records (for example: "Jewelry by Josephine, 1995 Volume"). Alternative title: If the work is known by two titles, you also may give the second title. If the work has been published as part of a larger work (including a periodical), give the title of that larger work instead of an alternative title.

2 Name and Address of Author/Owner of the Copyright

Give your name and mailing address. (You may include your pseudonym followed by "pseud.") Also, give the nation of which you are a citizen or where you have your domicile (i.e., permanent residence).
Please give daytime phone and fax numbers, if available.

with the application. For example, if you are registering illustrations but have not written the story yet, check only the box for "2-dimensional artwork".

6 Signature of Author

Sign the application in black ink.

7 Person to Contact for Rights and Permissions

This space is optional. You may give the name and address of the person or organization to contact for permission to use the work. You may also provide phone, fax, or e-mail information.

8 Mail Certificate to

This space must be completed. Your certificate of registration will be mailed in a window envelope to this address. Also, if the Copyright Office needs to contact you, we will write to this address.

3 Year of Creation

Give the year in which you completed the work you are registering at this time. (A work is "created" when it is "fixed" in a tangible form. Examples: drawn on paper, molded in clay, stored in a computer.)

4 Publication

If the work has been published (i.e., if copies have been distributed to the public), give the complete date of publication (month, day, and year) and the nation where the publication first took place.

5 Type of Authorship in This Work

Check the box or boxes that describe the kind of material you are registering. Check *only* the authorship included in the copy you are sending.

MAIL WITH THE FORM—

• a $20.00 filing fee in the form of a check or money order (*no cash*) payable to "Register of Copyrights," **and**
• one or two copies of the work or identifying material consisting of photographs or drawings showing the work. See table below for the requirements for most works. **Note:** Inquire about the requirements for other works or for any work first published before 1978. Copies submitted become the property of the U.S. Government.

If you are registering	And the work is *unpublished,* send	And the work is *published,* send
2-dimensional artwork in a book, map, poster, or print	one complete copy or identifying material	two copies of the best published edition
3-dimensional sculpture, T-shirt design	identifying material	identifying material
a greeting card, pattern, commercial print or label, fabric, wallpaper	one complete copy or identifying material	one copy of the best published edition

Mail everything (**application form, copy or copies, and fee) *in one package* to: Register of Copyrights
Library of Congress
Washington, D.C. 20559-6000

9 Deposit Account

Complete this space only if you currently maintain a deposit account in the Copyright Office.

Questions? Call (202) 707-3000 between 8:30 a.m. and 5:00 p.m. Eastern Time, Monday through Friday. For forms, call (202) 707-9100 24 hours a day, 7 days a week.

APPENDIX G:

Circular 40a: Deposit Requirements for Registration of Claims to Copyright in Visual Arts Material

40a

Deposit Requirements for Registration of Claims to Copyright in Visual Arts Material

IN GENERAL

To register a claim to copyright in a work of the visual arts, submit a properly completed application Form VA, a nonrefundable filing fee of $20.00, and an appropriate deposit, generally one complete copy of the work if unpublished, two complete copies of the best edition if the work was first published in the United States, or, for certain types of works, identifying material instead of actual copies.

This circular presents a simplified version of the deposit requirements for registration of claims to copyright in visual arts material. It should be viewed only as a basic guide. The items given on pages 3 and 4 are only examples and are not meant to be restrictive. For more detailed information, write for a copy of Circular 96, Sections 202.19, 202.20, and 202.21, which contains the deposit regulations of the Copyright Office. (See "For More Information" on back page.)

a work in the form of photographic prints, transparencies, photocopies, or drawings that show the complete copyrightable content of the work being registered.

SPECIFICATIONS FOR VISUAL ARTS IDENTIFYING MATERIAL

Copyright Office regulations require the deposit of identifying material instead of copies for three-dimensional works and for works that have been applied to three-dimensional objects. Examples of such works include sculpture, toys, jewelry, artwork on plates, and fabric or textile attached to or part of a three-dimensional object such as furniture. Identifying material must also be submitted for any pictorial, graphic, or sculptural work that exceeds 96 inches in any dimension.

In certain cases, identifying material is permitted; in other cases, it is required. (See chart on pages 3 and 4.) Identifying material should meet the following specifications:

BASIC DEFINITIONS

Complete Copy

A "complete copy" of an **unpublished** work is a copy that represents the complete copyrightable content of the work being registered. A complete copy of a **published** work is one that contains all elements of the unit of publication, including those which, if considered separately, would not be copyrightable subject matter. The copies deposited for registration should be physically undamaged.

Best Edition

The "best edition" is the edition published in the United States at any time before the date of deposit in the Copyright Office that the Library of Congress determines to be most suitable for its purposes. Generally, when more than one edition is available, the best edition is: larger rather than smaller; color rather than black and white; and printed on archival-quality rather than less-permanent paper. Request Circular 7b, "'Best Edition' of Published Copyrighted Works for the Collections of the Library of Congress," for additional information.

Identifying Material (I.D. Material)

"Identifying material" or "I.D. material" generally consists of two-dimensional reproduction(s) or rendering(s) of

- **Type of identifying material:** The material should consist of photographic prints, transparencies, photocopies, drawings, or similar two-dimensional reproductions or renderings of the work, in a form visually perceivable without the aid of a machine or device.
- **Color or black and white:** If the work is a pictorial or graphic work, the material should reproduce the actual colors employed in the work. In all other cases, the material may be in black and white or may consist of a reproduction of the actual colors.
- **Completeness:** As many pieces of identifying material should be submitted as are necessary to show clearly the entire copyrightable content of the work for which registration is being sought.
- **Number of sets:** Only one set of complete identifying material is required. **NOTE:** With respect to three-dimensional holograms, please write the Copyright Office for additional information.
- **Size:** Photographic transparencies must be at least 35 mm in size and, if 3 x 3 inches or less, must be fixed in cardboard, plastic, or similar mounts; transparencies larger than 3 x 3 inches should be mounted. All types of identifying material other than photographic transparencies must be not less than 3 x 3 inches and not more than 9 x 12 inches, but preferably 8 x 10 inches. The image of the work should show clearly the entire copyrightable content of the work.

(continued on page 4)

TWO-DIMENSIONAL WORKS

Nature of Work	Required Deposit	
	Published	Unpublished
Advertisements (pictorial)	1 copy as published or prepublication camera-ready copy	1 photocopy, proof, drawing, copy, or layout
Artwork for bed, bath, and table linens or for wearing apparel (for example, heat transfers or decals already applied to T-shirts)	I.D. material preferred in all cases; I.D. material required if copy cannot be folded to 4" thickness or less; 1 copy permitted if it can be folded to 4" thickness or less	same as published
Blueprints, architectural drawings, mechanical drawings, diagrams	1 complete copy	1 copy
Book jackets or record jackets	1 complete copy	1 copy
Commercial print published in newspaper or other periodical	1 copy of entire page or pages	

TWO-DIMENSIONAL WORKS (continued)

Nature of Work	Required Deposit	
	Published	Unpublished
Fabric emblems or patches, decals or heat transfers (not applied to clothing), bumper stickers, campaign buttons	1 complete copy	1 copy or I.D. material
Greeting cards, picture postcards, stationery, business cards, calendars	1 complete copy	1 copy or I.D. material
Holograms	1 actual copy if image is visible without the aid of a machine or device; otherwise 2 sets of display instructions and 2 sets of I.D. material showing the displayed image	1 copy or display instructions and I.D. material of image
Maps or cartographic material	1 copy of CD-ROM if work published in that format; otherwise, 2	1 copy of CD-ROM if work fixed in that format; otherwise, 1 complete copy or

Type of work	Deposit		complete copies	I.D. material
Commercial print or label (for example, flyers, labels, brochures, or catalogs used in connection with the sale of goods or services)	1 complete copy	1 copy		
Patterns, cross-stitch graphs, stitchery brochures, needlework and craft kits			1 complete copy	1 copy or I.D. material
Contributions to collective works (photographs, drawings, cartoons, etc., published as part of a periodical or anthology)	1 complete copy of the best edition of entire collective work, complete section containing contribution if published in newspaper, entire page containing contribution, contribution cut from the newspaper, or photocopy of contribution as it was published			
Pictorial or graphic works (for example, artwork, drawings, illustrations, paintings)			2 complete copies	1 copy or I.D. material
Pictorial or graphic works fixed only in machine readable form			I.D. material	I.D. material
Posters, photographs, prints, brochures, exhibition catalogs			2 complete copies	1 copy or proof, photocopy, contact sheet
"Limited edition" posters, prints, or etchings (published in quantities of fewer than 5 copies, or 300 or fewer numbered copies if individual author is owner of copyright)			1 copy or I.D. material	
Fabric, textile, wallpaper, carpeting, floor tile, wrapping paper, yard goods (If applied to a three-dimensional work, see p. 4)	1 complete copy (or swatch) showing the design repeat and copyright notice, if any	1 complete copy (or I.D. material if the work has not been fixed in repeat)		
Oversize material (exceeding 96" in any dimension)			I.D. material	I.D. material

(If applied to a three-dimensional work, see p. 4)

THREE-DIMENSIONAL WORKS

Nature of Work	Required Deposit	
	Published	Unpublished
Artwork or illustrations on 3-D objects (for example, artwork on plates, mugs)	I.D. material	I.D. material
Fabric or textile attached to or part of a 3-D object (such as furniture)	I.D. material	I.D. material
Games	1 complete copy if container is no larger than 12"x24"x6"; otherwise, I.D. material	1 copy if container is no larger than 12"x24"x6"or I.D. material*
Globes, relief models, or relief maps	1 complete copy including the stand (I.D. material *not* acceptable)	1 complete copy or I. D. material*
Jewelry	I.D. material or 1 copy if fixed only in the form of jewelry cast in base metal not exceeding 4" in any dimension	same as published
Pictorial matter and/or text on a box or container that can be flattened (contents of container are not claimed)	1 copy of box or container if it can be flattened or 1 paper label	1 copy or I. D. material*
Prints or labels inseparable from a three-dimensional object (for example, silk screen label on a bottle)	I.D. material	I. D. material
Sculptures, toys, dolls, molds, relief plaques, statues	I.D. material	I. D. material
Sculpture (for example, doll) in a box with copyrightable pictorial and/or textual material; claim in sculpture and artwork/ text	I.D. material for sculpture plus 1 copy of box and any other printed material	I. D. material for sculpture plus copy of box or I.D. material*
Oversize material (exceeding 96" in any dimension)	I. D. material	I.D. material

* Because storage space is limited, the Copyright Office prefers I.D. material rather than a copy in these cases.

Copyright Office • Library of Congress

September 1996—75,000   ✪ PRINTED ON RECYCLED PAPER

ARCHITECTURAL WORKS

	Required Deposit	
	Unconstructed Building	Constructed Building
To be eligible for copyright protection, an architectural work must have been created on or after December 1, 1990, or have been unconstructed and embodied only in unpublished drawings as of that date. (Request Circular 41, "Copyright Claims in Architectural Works," for more information.)	1 complete copy of an architectural drawing or blueprint showing the overall form of the building and any interior arrangement of spaces and/or design elements in which copyright is claimed.	1 complete copy as described at left plus I.D. material in the form of photographs clearly identifying the architectural work being registered.

(continued from page 2)

● **Title and dimension:** At least one piece of identifying material must give the title of the work on its front, back, or mount and should include an exact measurement of one or more dimensions of the work.

Copyright Notice

For a work published with notice of copyright, the notice and its position on the work must be clearly shown on at least one piece of identifying material. If necessary because of the size or position of the notice, a separate drawing or similar reproduction may be submitted. Such reproduction should be no smaller than 3 x 3 inches and no larger than 9 x 12 inches and should show the exact appearance and content of the notice and its specific position on the work. For further information about the copyright notice, request Circular 3, "Copyright Notice."

FOR MORE INFORMATION

For publications, call the Forms and Publications Hotline, (202)707-9100 (24 hours a day), or write to the address below. Publications are also available via Fax-on-Demand and the Internet. See pages 2 and 3 for more information.

To speak with an information specialist or to request further information, call (202)707-3000 (TTY: (202) 707-6737) Monday-Friday, 8:30 a.m. to 5:00 p.m., Eastern Time, except Federal holidays, or write:

Copyright Office
Information Section, LM-455
Library of Congress
Washington, D.C. 20559-6000

● **Washington, D.C. 20559-6000**

☆U.S. GOVERNMENT PRINTING OFFICE: 1996-405-104/40,027

APPENDIX H:
Copyright Registration for Works of the Visual Arts

United States Copyright Office

Copyright

Registration

for Works

of the

Visual Arts

GENERAL INFORMATION

Copyright is a form of protection provided by the laws of the United States to the authors of "original works of authorship," including "pictorial, graphic, and sculptural works." The owner of copyright in a work has the exclusive right to make copies, to prepare derivative works, to sell or distribute copies, and to display the work publicly. Anyone else wishing to use the work in these ways must have the permission of the author or someone who has derived rights through the author.

Copyright Protection Is Automatic

Under the present copyright law, which became effective Jan. 1, 1978, a work is automatically protected by copyright when it is created. A work is created when it is "fixed" in a copy or phonorecord for the first time. Neither registration in the Copyright Office nor publication is required for copyright protection under the present law.

Advantages to Copyright Registration

There are, however, certain advantages to registration, including the establishment of a public record of the copyright claim. Copyright registration must generally be made before an infringement suit may be brought. Timely registration may also provide a broader range of remedies in an infringement suit.

Copyright Notice

Before March 1, 1989, the use of a copyright notice was mandatory on all published works, and any work first published before that date should have carried a notice. For works first published on or after March 1, 1989, use of the copyright notice is optional. For more information about copyright notice, request Circular 3, "Copyright Notice."

PUBLICATION

The copyright law defines "publication" as: the distribution of copies of a work to the public by sale or other transfer of ownership or by rental, lease, or lending. Offering to distribute copies to a group of persons for purposes of further distribution or public display also constitutes publication. A public display does not of itself constitute publication.

A work of art that exists in only one copy, such as a painting or statue, is not regarded as published when the single existing copy is sold or offered for sale in the traditional way, for example, through an art dealer, gallery, or auction house. A statue erected in a public place is not necessarily published.

When the work is reproduced in multiple copies (such as reproductions of a painting or castings of a statue), the work is published when the reproductions are publicly distributed or offered to a group for further distribution or public display.

Publication is an important concept in copyright because, among other reasons, whether a work is published or not may affect the number of copies and the type of material that must be deposited when registering the work. In addition, some works published in the United States become subject to mandatory deposit in the Library of Congress. These requirements are explained elsewhere in this circular.

WORKS OF THE VISUAL ARTS

Copyright protects original "pictorial, graphic, and sculptural works," which include two-dimensional and three-dimensional works of fine, graphic, and applied art. The following is a list of examples of such works:[1]

- Advertisements, commercial prints, labels

- Artificial flowers and plants

- Artwork applied to clothing or to other useful articles

- Bumper stickers, decals, stickers

- Cartographic works, such as maps, globes, relief models

- Cartoons, comic strips

- Collages

- Dolls, toys

- Drawings, paintings, murals

- Enamel works

- Fabric, floor, and wallcovering designs

- Games, puzzles

- Greeting cards, postcards, stationery

- Holograms, computer and laser artwork

- Jewelry designs

- Models

- Mosaics

- Needlework and craft kits

- Original prints, such as engravings, etchings, serigraphs, silk screen prints, woodblock prints

- Patterns for sewing, knitting, crochet, needlework

- Photographs, photomontages

- Posters

- Record jacket artwork or photography

- Relief and intaglio prints

- Reproductions, such as lithographs, collotypes

- Sculpture, such as carvings, ceramics, figurines, maquettes, molds, relief sculptures

- Stained glass designs

- Stencils, cut-outs

- Technical drawings, architectural drawings or plans, blueprints, diagrams, mechanical drawings

- Weaving designs, lace designs, tapestries

[1] Copyright protection extends to the design of a building created for the use of human beings. Architectural works created on or after Dec.1, 1990, or that on Dec. 1, 1990, were either unconstructed or embodied only in unpublished plans or drawings are eligible. For registration of architectural works, use Form VA. Request Circular 41, "Copyright Claims in Architectural Works," for more information.

Copyright protection for an original work of authorship does not extend to the following:

- Ideas, concepts, discoveries, principles

- Formulas, processes, systems, methods, procedures

- Words and short phrases, such as names, titles, and slogans

- Familiar symbols or designs

- Mere variations of typographic ornamentation, lettering, or coloring

USEFUL ARTICLES

A "useful article" is an article having an intrinsic utilitarian function that is not merely to portray the appearance of the article or to convey information. Examples are clothing, furniture, machinery, dinnerware, and lighting fixtures. An article that is normally part of a useful article may itself be a useful article, for example, an ornamental wheel cover on a vehicle.

Copyright does not protect the mechanical or utilitarian aspects of such works of craftsmanship. It may, however, protect any pictorial, graphic, or sculptural authorship that can be identified separately from the utilitarian aspects of an object. Thus, a useful article may have both copyrightable and uncopyrightable features. For example, a carving on the back of a chair or a floral relief design on silver flatware could be protected by copyright, but the design of the chair or flatware itself could not.

Some designs of useful articles may qualify for protection under the federal patent law. For further information, contact the Patent and Trademark Office at Commissioner of Patents and Trademarks, Washington, D.C. 20231 or via the Internet at http://www.uspto.gov. The telephone number is (800) 786-9199 and the TTY number is (703) 305-7785. The automated information line is (703) 308-4357.

Copyright in a work that portrays a useful article extends only to the artistic expression of the author of the pictorial, graphic, or sculptural work. It does not extend to the design of the article that is portrayed. For example, a drawing or photograph of an automobile or a dress design may be copyrighted, but that does not give the artist or photographer the exclusive right to make automobiles or dresses of the same design.

REGISTRATION PROCEDURES

If you choose to register a claim in your work, package together the following materials in the same envelope:

1. A properly completed application form

2. A nonreturnable deposit of the work to be registered, and

3. A nonrefundable filing fee of $20* in the form of a check or money order payable to the **Register of Copyrights** with each application

> *NOTE: Filing fees are effective through June 30, 1999. For the most current fee information, please write the Copyright Office, check the Copyright Office Website at http://www.loc.gov/copyright, or call (202) 707-3000.

Send the items to:
Library of Congress
Copyright Office
101 Independence Ave., S.E.
Washington, D.C. 20559-6000

Application Form

Form VA is the appropriate form for registration of a work of the visual arts. The form should be completed legibly with black ink or type. Do not use pencil or send a carbon copy. All pertinent information should be given on the basic application form.

If you photocopy our forms, be sure that they are legible and printed head-to-head so that when you turn the sheet over, the top of page 2 is directly behind the top of page 1. Do not send two-page photocopies. The application must bear an original signature in ink. A continuation sheet supplied by the Copyright Office should be used only when all necessary information cannot be recorded on the basic form. No other attachments will be accepted. For information on ordering application forms and circulars, see "For Further Information" on page 6 of this circular.

DEPOSIT REQUIREMENTS

Circular 40a, "Deposit Requirements for Registration of Claims to Copyright in Visual Arts Material," provides a basic guide about material that should be sent when registering a claim. Circular 40a also defines basic terms such as "complete copy," "best edition," and "identifying material." The following is a general outline of the deposit requirements:

Two-Dimensional Works

If unpublished, send one complete copy or identifying material.

If first published in the United States **on or after** Jan. 1, 1978, generally send two complete copies of the best edition.

If first published in the United States **before** Jan. 1, 1978, send two complete copies of the best edition as first published. Where identifying material is permitted or required, the identifying material must represent the work as first published.

If first published outside the United States **before March 1, 1989,** send one complete copy of the work as first published. Where identifying material is permitted or required, the identifying material must represent the work as first published.

If first published outside the United States **after March 1, 1989,** send one complete copy of either the first published edition or the best edition of the work.

Three-Dimensional Works and Two-Dimensional Works Applied to Three-Dimensional Objects

For published and unpublished works, send identifying material, such as photographs. **Do not** send the three-dimensional work.

Special Provisions

For some works first published in the United States, only **one copy** is required instead of two. These include:

- Greeting cards, picture postcards, stationery, business cards

- Games

- Pictorial matter or text on a box or container (where the contents of the container are not claimed)

- Contributions to collective works. The deposit may be either one complete copy of the best edition of the entire collective work, the complete section containing the contribution, the contribution cut from the collective work in which it appeared, or a photocopy of the contribution itself as it was published in the collective work.

For some works, identifying material is permitted, not required. For example, either identifying material or actual copies may be deposited for some unpublished works and for limited editions of posters or prints with certain qualifying conditions.

For all works that exceed 96 inches in any dimension, identifying material is required.

For additional information on what is permitted or required for registration of certain kinds of visual arts works, request Circular 40a and Circular 96, Sections 202.19, 20, and 21, which contains the deposit regulations of the Copyright Office.

Deposits cannot be returned.

REGISTRATION FOR TWO OR MORE WORKS WITH ONE APPLICATION AND FEE

Two or more individual works may be registered with one application and fee as follows:

Unpublished Works

A group of unpublished works may be registered as a collection if **all** the following conditions are met.

- The elements of the collection are assembled in an orderly form.

- The combined elements bear a single title identifying the collection as a whole.

- The copyright claimant or claimants for each element in the collection are the same.

- All the elements are by the same author, or if they are by different authors, at least one author has contributed copyrightable authorship to each element.

NOTE: Works registered as an unpublished collection will be listed in the records of the Copyright Office only under the collection title.

Published Works

All copyrightable elements that are included in a single unit of publication and in which the copyright claimant is the same may be considered a single work for registration purposes. An example is a game consisting of playing pieces, a game board, and game instructions.

Group Registration of Contributions to Periodicals

A single registration may be made for a group of contributions to periodicals if **all** the following conditions are met.

- All the works have the same copyright claimant.

- All the works are by the same author.

- The author of each work is an individual, not an employer or other person for whom the work was made for hire.

- Each work was first published as a contribution to a periodical (including newspapers) within a 12-month period.

- The application identifies each contribution separately, including the periodical containing it and the date of its first publication.

In addition to the above conditions, if first published before March 1, 1989, a contribution as first published must have borne a separate copyright notice, and the name of the owner of copyright in the work (or an abbreviation or alternative designation of the owner) must have been the same in each notice.

Such contributions are registered on Form VA accompanied by Form GR/CP (group registration of contributions to periodicals). Examples of works eligible for such a group registration include cartoon strips, newspaper columns, horoscopes, photographs, drawings, and illustrations.

No Blanket Protection

Registration covers only the particular work deposited for the registration. It does not give any sort of "blanket" protection to other works in the same series. For example, registration of a single cartoon or comic strip drawing does not cover any earlier or later drawings. Each copyrightable version or issue must be registered to gain the advantages of registration for the new material it contains. However, under the conditions described above under **"Published Works"** and **"Group Registration of Contributions to Periodicals,"** certain group registrations may be made with one application and fee.

MANDATORY DEPOSIT FOR WORKS PUBLISHED IN THE UNITED STATES

Although a copyright registration is not required, the 1976 Copyright Act establishes a mandatory deposit requirement for works published in the United States. In general, the owner of copyright or the owner of the exclusive right of publication in the work has a legal obligation to deposit in the Copyright Office within 3 months of publication in the United States **two** complete copies or phonorecords of the best edition. It is the responsibility of the owner of copyright or the owner of the right of first publication in the work to fulfill this mandatory deposit requirement. Failure to make the deposit can result in fines and other penalties but does not affect copyright protection.

Some categories of pictorial, graphic, and sculptural works are exempt from this requirement, and the obligation is reduced for other categories. The following works are **exempt** from the mandatory deposit requirement:

- Scientific and technical drawings and models

- Greeting cards, picture postcards, and stationery

- Three dimensional sculptural works, except for globes, relief models, and similar cartographic works

- Works published only as reproduced in or on jewelry, toys, games, textiles, packaging material, and any useful article

- Advertising material published in connection with articles of merchandise, works of authorship, or services

- Works first published as individual contributions to collective works (but not the collective work as a whole)

- Works first published outside the United States and later published without change in the United States, under certain conditions (**see** Circular 96, Sections 202.19, 20, and 21)

Copies deposited for the Library of Congress under the mandatory deposit provision may also be used to register the claim to copyright but only if they are accompanied by the prescribed application and fee for registration. For further information about mandatory deposit, request Circular 7d, "Mandatory Deposit of Copies or Phonorecords for the Library of Congress."

EFFECTIVE DATE OF REGISTRATION

A copyright registration is effective on the date the Copyright Office receives all the required elements in acceptable form, regardless of how long it then takes to process the application and mail the certificate of registration. The time the Copyright Office requires to process an application varies, depending on the amount of material the Office is receiving.

If you apply for copyright registration, you will not receive an acknowledgment that your application has been received (the Office receives more than 600,000 applications annually), but you can expect

- A letter or a telephone call from a Copyright Office staff member if further information is needed or

- A certificate of registration indicating that the work has been registered, or if the application cannot be accepted, a letter explaining why it has been rejected.

If you want to know the date that the Copyright Office receives your material, send it by registered or certified mail and request a return receipt.

MORAL RIGHTS FOR VISUAL ARTISTS

For certain one-of-a-kind visual art and numbered limited editions of 200 or fewer copies, authors are accorded rights of attribution and integrity. The right of attribution ensures that artists are correctly identified with the works of art they create and that they are not identified with works created by others. The right of integrity allows artists to protect their works against modifications and destructions that are prejudicial to the artists' honor or reputation. These rights may not be transferred by the author, but they may be waived in a written instrument. Transfer of the physical copy of a work of visual art or of the copyright does not affect the moral rights accorded to the author.

For works of visual art incorporated in a building, special rules apply. If the owner of a building desires to remove such a work from the building and removal is possible without destruction, the owner is required to accord the author the opportunity to make the removal himself. A registry is established within the Copyright Office to record information relevant to this obligation. Both owners of buildings and authors of visual art incorporated in buildings may record statements in the registry. For further information, request Circular 96, Section 201.25, "Visual Arts Registry."

FOR FURTHER INFORMATION

To request Copyright Office circulars and application forms, write to:

Library of Congress
Copyright Office
Publications Section, LM-455
101 Independence Ave., S.E.
Washington, D.C. 20559-6000

Or, if you know which circulars you want, request them from the **Forms and Publications Hotline** at (202) 707-9100 24 hours a day. Leave a recorded message.

Selected circulars and other information (but not application forms) are available from **Fax-On-Demand** at (202) 707-2600.

Circulars, announcements, regulations, related material, and all copyright application forms are available via the Copyright Office **Website** at http://www.loc.gov/copyright.

For general information about copyright, call the **Copyright Public Information Office** at (202) 707-3000. The TTY number is (202) 707-6737.

Library of Congress • Copyright Office • 101 Independence Ave., S.E. • Washington, D.C. 20559-6000
http://www.loc.gov/copyright

March 1998–50,000   ♻ PRINTED ON RECYCLED PAPER   ☆ U.S. GOVERNMENT PRINTING OFFICE: 1998: 432-381/60,040

APPENDIX I:
New York Living Will (Sample)

New York Living Will

This Living Will has been prepared to conform to the law in the State of New York, as set forth in the case In re Westchester County Medical Center, 72 N.Y.2d 517 (1988). In that case the Court established the need for "clear and convincing" evidence of a patient's wishes and stated that the "ideal situation is one in which the patient's wishes were expressed in some form of writing, perhaps a 'living will.'"

PRINT YOUR NAME

I, _____, being of sound mind, make this statement as a directive to be followed if I become permanently unable to participate in decisions regarding my medical care. These instructions reflect my firm and settled commitment to decline medical treatment under the circumstances indicated below:

I direct my attending physician to withhold or withdraw treatment that merely prolongs my dying, if I should be in an **incurable or irreversible mental or physical condition with no reasonable expectation of recovery,** including but not limited to: (a) **a terminal condition;** (b) **a**

permanently unconscious condition; or (c) **a minimally conscious condition in which I am permanently unable to make decisions or express my wishes.**

I direct that my treatment be limited to measures to keep me comfortable and to relieve pain, including any pain that might occur by withholding or withdrawing treatment.

While I understand that I am not legally required to be specific about future treatments **if I am in the condition(s) described above I feel especially strongly about the following forms of treatment:**

I do not want cardiac resuscitation.
I do not want mechanical respiration.
I do not want artificial nutrition and hydration.
I do not want antibiotics.

However, I **do want** maximum pain relief, even if it may hasten my death.

NOTE:
We strongly advise using documents specific to the state in which one resides.

ADD PERSONAL INSTRUCTIONS (IF ANY)

Other directions:

These directions express my legal right to refuse treatment, under the law of New York. I intend my instructions to be carried out, unless I have rescinded them in a new writing or by clearly indicating that I have changed my mind.

SIGN AND DATE THE DOCUMENT AND PRINT YOUR ADDRESS

Signed _____ Date _____

Address _____

I declare that the person who signed this document appeared to execute the living will willingly and free from duress. He or she signed (or asked another to sign for him or her) this document in my presence.

Witness 1 _____

Address _____

Witness 2 _____

Address _____

Courtesy of **Choice In Dying, Inc.**
1035 30th Street, NW Washington, DC 20007 800-989-9455

6/96

APPENDIX J:
New York Health Care Proxy (Sample)

New York
Health Care Proxy

PRINT YOUR
NAME

PRINT NAME,
HOME ADDRESS
AND
TELEPHONE
NUMBER OF
YOUR AGENT

(1) I, _____, hereby appoint:

(name)

_____

_____

(name, home address and telephone number of agent)

as my health care agent to make any and all health care decisions for me, except to the extent that I state otherwise.

This Health Care Proxy shall take effect in the event I become unable to make my own health care decisions.

(2) Optional instructions: I direct my agent to make health care decisions in accord with my wishes and limitations as stated below, or as he or she otherwise knows.

NOTE: We strongly advise using documents specific to the state in which one resides.

(Unless your agent knows your wishes about artificial nutrition and hydration [feeding tubes], your agent will not be allowed to make decisions about artificial nutrition and hydration.)

(3) Name of substitute or fill-in agent if the person I appoint above is unable, unwilling or unavailable to act as my health care agent.

_____

_____
(name, home address and telephone number of alternate agent)

_____

PRINT NAME, HOME ADDRESS AND TELEPHONE NUMBER OF YOUR ALTERNATE AGENT

(4) Unless I revoke it, this proxy shall remain in effect indefinitely, or until the date or condition I have stated below. This proxy shall expire (specific date or conditions, if desired): _____

_____

ENTER A DURATION OR A CONDITION (IF ANY)

(5) Signature _____ Date _____

Address _____

SIGN AND DATE THE DOCUMENT AND PRINT YOUR ADDRESS

Statement by Witnesses (must be 18 or older)

I declare that the person who signed this document appeared to execute the proxy willingly and free from duress. He or she signed (or asked another to sign for him or her) this document in my presence. I am not the person appointed as proxy by this document.

Witness 1 _____

Address _____

Witness 2 _____

Address _____

WITNESSING PROCEDURE

YOUR WITNESSES MUST SIGN AND PRINT THEIR ADDRESSES

APPENDIX K:

Durable General Power of Attorney—New York Statutory Short Form

Blumberg Excelsior, Inc.
Publisher, NYC 10013

M 51 — Statutory short form of General Power of Attorney:
with affidavit of attorney, GOL § 5-1501; 12 pt. type, 1-97

Blumbergs
Law Products

DURABLE GENERAL POWER OF ATTORNEY

NEW YORK STATUTORY SHORT FORM

THE POWERS YOU GRANT BELOW CONTINUE TO BE EFFECTIVE

SHOULD YOU BECOME DISABLED OR INCOMPETENT

Caution: This is an important document. It gives the person whom you designate (your "Agent") broad powers to handle your property during your lifetime, which may include powers to mortgage, sell, or otherwise dispose of any real or personal property without advance notice to you or approval by you. These powers will continue to exist even after you become disabled or incompetent. These powers are explained more fully in New York General Obligations Law, Article 5, Title 15, Sections 5-1502A through 5-1503, which expressly permit the use of any other or different form of power of attorney.

This document does not authorize anyone to make medical or other health care decisions. You may execute a health care proxy to do this.

If there is anything about this form that you do not understand, you should ask a lawyer to explain it to you.

THIS is intended to constitute a DURABLE GENERAL POWER OF ATTORNEY pursuant to Article 5, Title 15 of the New York General Obligations Law:

I,

do hereby appoint:

(insert your name and address)

(If 1 person is to be appointed agent, insert the name and address of your agent above)

(If 2 or more persons are to be appointed agents by you insert their names and addresses above)

my attorney(s)-in-fact TO ACT

(If more than one agent is designated, CHOOSE ONE of the following two choices by putting your initials in ONE of the blank spaces to the left of your choice:)

[   ] Each agent may SEPARATELY act.

[   ] All agents must act TOGETHER.

(If neither blank space is initialed, the agents will be required to act TOGETHER)

IN MY NAME, PLACE AND STEAD in any way which I myself could do, if I were personally present, with respect to the following matters as each of them is defined in Title 15 of Article 5 of the New York General Obligations Law to the extent that I am permitted by law to act through an agent:

(DIRECTIONS: Initial in the blank space to the left of your choice any one or more of the following lettered subdivisions as to which you WANT to give your agent authority. If the blank space to the left of any particular lettered subdivision is NOT initialed, NO AUTHORITY WILL BE GRANTED for matters that are included in that subdivision. Alternatively, the letter corresponding to each power you wish to grant may be written or typed on the blank line in subdivision "(Q)", and you may then put your initials in the blank space to the left of subdivision "(Q)" in order to grant each of the powers so indicated.)

[   ] (A) real estate transactions;

[   ] (B) chattel and goods transactions;

[   ] (C) bond, share and commodity
transactions;

[   ] (D) banking transactions;

[   ] (E) business operating transactions;

[   ] (F) insurance transactions;

[   ] (G) estate transactions;

[   ] (H) claims and litigation;

[   ] (I) personal relationships and affairs;

[   ] (J) benefits from military service;

[   ] (K) records, reports and statements;

[   ] (L) retirement benefit transactions;

[   ] (M) making gifts to my spouse, children
and more remote descendants,
and parents, not to exceed in the
aggregate $10,000 to each of such
persons in any year;

[   ] (N) tax matters;

[   ] (O) all other matters

[   ] (P) full and unqualified authority to my
attorney(s)-in-fact to delegate any
or all of the foregoing powers to
any person or persons whom my
attorney(s)-in-fact shall select;

[   ] (Q) each of the above matters identified
by the following letters: ....

....

This Durable Power of Attorney shall not be affected by my subsequent disability or incompetence.

If every agent named above is unable or unwilling to serve, I appoint

(insert name and address of successor)

to be my agent for all purposes hereunder.

To induce any third party to act hereunder, I hereby agree that any third party receiving a duly executed copy or facsimile of this instrument may act hereunder, and that revocation or termination hereof shall be ineffective as to such third party unless and until actual notice or knowledge of such revocation or termination shall have been received by such third party, and I for myself and for my heirs, executors, legal representatives and assigns, hereby agree to indemnify and hold harmless any such third party from and against any and all claims that may arise against such third party by reason of such third party having relied on the provisions of this instrument.

This Durable General Power of Attorney may be revoked by me at any time.

In Witness Whereof, I have hereunto signed my name this   day of

(YOU SIGN HERE:) ➡

_____

(Signature of Principal)

ACKNOWLEDGEMENTS

STATE OF   ss.:

COUNTY OF

On   before me personally came

_____

to me known, and known to me to be the individual   described in, and who executed the foregoing instrument, and   he   acknowledged to me that   he   executed the same.

STATE OF   ss.:

COUNTY OF

On   before me personally came

_____

to me known, and known to me to be the individual   described in, and who executed the foregoing instrument, and   he   acknowledged to me that   he   executed the same.

AFFIDAVIT THAT POWER OF ATTORNEY IS IN FULL FORCE

(Sign before a notary public)

STATE OF   COUNTY OF   ss.:

            being duly sworn, deposes and says:

1. The Principal within did, in writing, appoint me as the Principal's true and lawful ATTORNEY(S)-IN-FACT in the within Power of Attorney.

2. I have no actual knowledge or actual notice of revocation or termination of the Power of Attorney by death or otherwise, or knowledge of any facts indicating the same. I further represent that the Principal is alive, has not revoked or repudiated the Power of Attorney and the Power of Attorney still is in full force and effect.

3. I make this affidavit for the purpose of inducing

to accept delivery of the following Instrument(s), as executed by me in my capacity as the ATTORNEY(S)-IN-FACT, with full knowledge that this affidavit will be relied upon in accepting the execution and delivery of the Instrument(s) and in paying good and valuable consideration therefor:

_____

Sworn to before me on

TO

DURABLE

Power of Attorney
Statutory Short Form

Dated,

APPENDIX L:
Power of Attorney

Blumbergs Law Products

P 3130—Power of attorney (simple, durable or springing),
with affidavit that power is in full force. 9-94

© 1987 BY JULIUS BLUMBERG, INC.
PUBLISHER, NYC 10013

Consult your Lawyer before signing this document. It has important legal consequences.

Power of Attorney

1. Grantor of the Power of Attorney, and address:

2. Attorney, and address:

(The words Grantor and Attorney shall include all grantors and all attorneys under this Power of Attorney)

3. Creation of the Power of Attorney

The Grantor hereby appoints the Attorney as the true and lawful attorney in fact of the Grantor for the Purposes stated in this Power of Attorney. The Attorney is granted full power and authority to the extent permitted by law to do whatever is necessary to achieve the Purposes as the Grantor personally could do.

4. Purposes: All of the following purposes except those stricken are included in this Power of Attorney.

To strike out any purpose the Grantor must draw a line through the text of that subdivision AND initial within the brackets.

If any purposes are stricken, Grantor may wish to also strike out (M) all other matters.

(A) real estate transactions; .... [   ]   [   ]   *(I) personal relationships and affairs;* .... [   ]

(B) *chattel and goods transactions;* ...... [   ]
(C) *bond, share and commodity transactions;* ...... [   ]
(D) *banking transactions;* ...... [   ]
(E) *business operating transactions;* ...... [   ]
(F) *insurance transactions;* ...... [   ]
(G) *estate transactions;* ...... [   ]
(H) *claims and litigation;* ...... [   ]

(J) *benefits from military service;* ...... [   ]
(K) *records, reports and statements;* ...... [   ]
(L) *full and unqualified authority to the Attorney to delegate any or all of the foregoing powers to any person or persons whom the Attorney shall select;* ...... [   ]
(M) *all other matters;* ...... [   ]

5. Substitution and Revocation *(Delete if purpose [L] is stricken.)*

The Attorney shall have full power of substitution and revocation. This means that the Attorney may appoint another to act under this Power of Attorney, and to revoke that appointment.

6. Durable Power

This Power of Attorney shall not be affected by the subsequent disability or incompetence of the Grantor.

7. Springing Power[1] *(If this space is left empty this Power of Attorney will not be a Springing Power of Attorney)*

8. Inducement of Third Parties to Act

Grantor agrees that any third party receiving a signed copy or reproduction of this Power of Attorney may act under it. Revocation or termination of this Power of Attorney will not be effective until the third party receives actual knowledge of the termination or revocation. Grantor shall hold harmless any third party from and against any claims that may arise against the third party as a result of reliance on this Power of Attorney.

In Witness Whereof, Grantor has signed this Power on _____ 19____

In the presence of:

_____ of _____
signature   address

_____ of _____
signature   address

STATE OF   COUNTY OF   ss.:

On _____ 19____ before me, the subscriber, personally appeared

to me personally known, and known to me to be the same person described in and who executed the foregoing Power of Attorney, and   he acknowledged to me that   he executed the same.

_____

Affidavit that Power of Attorney is in Full Force

STATE OF   COUNTY OF   ss.:

being duly sworn, deposes and says:

1. The Grantor within did, in writing, appoint me as the Grantor's true and lawful attorney in fact in the within Power of Attorney.

2. As Attorney for the Grantor and pursuant to the Power of Attorney, I have executed the following Instrument(s):

3. At the time I executed the Instrument(s) I had no actual knowledge or actual notice of revocation or termination of the Power of Attorney by death or otherwise, or knowledge of any facts indicating the same. I further represent that the Grantor is alive, has not revoked or repudiated the Power of Attorney and the Power of Attorney still is in full force and effect.

4. I make this affidavit for the purpose of inducing

to accept delivery of the Instrument(s), as executed by me in my capacity as the Attorney of the Grantor, with full knowledge that this affidavit will be relied upon in accepting the execution and delivery of the Instrument(s) and in paying good and valuable consideration therefor.

Sworn to before me on   19

_____

---

[1]If Grantor wishes the Power of Attorney to become effective only upon disability, and such Springing Power of Attorney is permitted in the jurisdiction, insert the following provision or other provision required in the jurisdiction:

This Power of Attorney shall become effective upon the disability of the Grantor whereby Grantor is unable to manage Grantor's property and affairs effectively. Such disability shall be deemed to exist and the Attorney may act pursuant to this Power of Attorney only after a licensed physician (you may give the name and address of a specific physician) has certified such disability in writing.

Note: If the principal wishes to allow the attorney to continue a pattern of gifts the principal has begun, add the following language after paragraph 8:

The attorney named herein has the power to make gifts in the pattern I have used in my lifetime.

APPENDIX M:
Living Will

WARNING: This document may not be legally binding. Consult an attorney as to its legal effect.

Living Will

To: My Family, my Physician, my Lawyer, my Clergyman, any Medical Facility in whose care I happen to be and any individual who may become responsible for my Health, Welfare or Affairs:

If the time comes when I can no longer take part in decisions concerning my life, I wish and direct the following:

If a situation should arise in which there is no reasonable expectation for my recovery from extreme physical or mental disability, I direct that I be allowed to die, and not be kept alive by medications, artificial means, life support equipment or "heroic measures". I do, however, ask that medication be mercifully administered to me to alleviate suffering even though this may shorten my remaining life.

This statement is made after careful consideration and is in accordance with my convictions and beliefs. I urge those concerned to take whatever action necessary, including legal action, to fulfill my wishes and directions. To the extent that the provisions of this document are not legally enforceable, I hope that those to whom it is addressed will regard themselves as morally bound by it.

Elective Provisions
Check the box and write initials next to each election you desire.

☐ .... 1. I wish to live out my last days at home rather than in a hospital if it does not jeopardize the chance of my recovery to a meaningful and conscious life and does not impose an undue burden on my family.

☐ 2. If any of my tissues or organs are sound and would be of value as transplants to other people, I freely give my permission for such donations.

In Witness Whereof, I state that I have read this, my living will, know and understand its contents and sign my name below.

Dated .... 19 ....

....
Signature

....
Print or type full name, address & tel. no. of person signing.

Witness* ....

....

Witness* ....

....

* After each witness signature print or type full name, address and tel. no.

Copies of this document have been given to the following:

Name _____

Name _____

Address _____

Telephone _____

Telephone _____

Your state may have specific rules regarding this living will such as how long it will be effective, requirements for witnesses, etc. Consult your attorney before signing.

Optional Acknowledgement

STATE OF

COUNTY OF ss.:

On _____ 19_____ before me personally came

Living Will
of

Dated_____19____

APPENDIX N:
Health Care Proxy (with living will directives)

M 95—Health care proxy with living will directives, PHL § 2980, 7-94

JULIUS BLUMBERG, INC.,
PUBLISHER, NYC 10013

Health Care Proxy

(with living will directives)

I .... hereby appoint
  Person giving this proxy

Agent

....
Name of agent

....
Home address

....
Telephone number of agent

as my health care agent to make any and all health care decisions for me, except to the extent
I state otherwise.

This health care proxy shall take effect in the event I become unable to make my own health care decisions.

NOTE: Although not necessary, and neither encouraged nor discouraged, you may wish to state instructions or wishes, and limit your agent's authority. Unless your agent knows your wishes about artificial nutrition and hydration, your agent will not have authority to decide about artificial nutrition and hydration. If you choose to state instructions, wishes, or limits, please do so below:

If a situation should arise in which there is no reasonable expectation for my recovery from extreme physical or mental disability, I direct that I be allowed to die, and not be kept alive by medications, artificial means, life support equipment or "heroic measures". I do, however, ask that medication be mercifully administered to me to alleviate suffering even though this may shorten my remaining life.

This statement is made after careful consideration and is in accordance with my convictions and beliefs. I urge those concerned to take whatever action necessary, including legal action, to fulfill my wishes and directions.

I additionally direct the following by checking the box and writing my initials next to the desired provisions.

☐ .... 1. I do not wish artificial nutrition.

☐ .... 2. I do not wish artificial hydration.

☐ .... 3. I wish to live out my last days at home rather than in a hospital if it does not jeopardize the chance of my recovery to a meaningful and conscious life and does not impose an undue burden on my family.

☐ .... 4. If any of my tissues or organs are sound and would be of value as transplants to other people, I freely give my permission for such donations.

☐ .... 5. ....

....

....

....

....

I DIRECT MY AGENT to make health care decisions in accordance with my wishes and instructions as stated above or as otherwise known to him or her. I also direct my agent to abide by any limitations on his or her authority as stated above or as otherwise known to him or her.

In the event the person I appoint above is unable, unwilling or unavailable to act as my health care agent, I hereby appoint

Alternate Agent

Name of agent
....

Home address
....

....

Telephone number of alternate agent
....

as my health care agent.

I UNDERSTAND THAT, unless I revoke it, this will remain in effect indefinitely or until the date or occurrence of the condition I have stated below:

*Please complete the following if you **DO NOT** want this health care proxy to be in effect indefinitely:*

This proxy shall expire:
....
Specify date or condition
....

Signature

.... Date

.... Address

I DECLARE THAT the person who signed or asked another to sign this document is personally known to me and appears to be of sound mind and acting willingly and free from duress. He or she signed (or asked another to sign for him or her) this document in my presence and that person signed in my presence. I am not the person appointed as agent by this document.

Witnesses

.... Date

.... Signature

.... Print name

.... Address

.... Zip Code

.... Telephone

.... Date

.... Signature

.... Print name

.... Address

.... Zip Code

.... Telephone

New York State PHL § 2980

Health Care Proxy

(with living will directives)

PUBLISHED BY
JULIUS BLUMBERG, INC., NYC 10013

Blumbergs
Law Products

....
Date of proxy

....
Person giving proxy

....
Agent

....
Alternate Agent

Publisher's Note: This Health Care Proxy is printed on 100% cotton content paper. Unlike ordinary photocopy paper, this quality stock resists turning brittle and brown with age. Insist on genuine Blumberg forms to ensure the longevity of this important document.

The publisher maintains property rights in the layout, graphic design and typestyle of this form as well as in the company's trademarked logo and name. Reproduction of blank copies of this form without the publisher's permission is prohibited. However, once a form has been filled in, photocopying is permitted.

APPENDIX O:
Health Care Proxy

P 70—Health care proxy, PHL § 2980, 4-91

Blumbergs
Law Products

Health Care Proxy

I _____ hereby appoint
Person giving this proxy

Agent

_____
Name of agent

_____
Home address

_____

_____
Telephone number of agent

as my health care agent to make any and all health care decisions for me, except to the extent I
state otherwise.

This health care proxy shall take effect in the event I become unable to make my own
health care decisions.

*NOTE: Although not necessary, and neither encouraged nor discouraged, you may wish to
state instructions or wishes, and limit your agent's authority. Unless your agent knows your
wishes about artificial nutrition and hydration, your agent will not have authority to decide
about artificial nutrition and hydration. If you choose to state instructions, wishes, or limits,
please do so below:*

I DIRECT MY AGENT to make health care decisions in accordance with my wishes and instructions as stated above or as otherwise known to him or her. I also direct my agent to abide by any limitations on his or her authority as stated above or as otherwise known to him or her.

In the event the person I appoint above is unable, unwilling or unavailable to act as my health care agent, I hereby appoint

Alternate
Agent

_____
Name of alternate agent

_____
Home address

_____
Telephone number of alternate agent

as my health care agent.

I UNDERSTAND THAT, unless I revoke it, this proxy will remain in effect indefinitely or until the date or occurrence of the condition I have stated below:

*Please complete the following if you **DO NOT** want this health care proxy to be in effect indefinitely:*

This proxy shall expire: ....
Specify date or condition

Signature ....
Date

Address ....

....

I DECLARE THAT the person who signed or asked another to sign this document is personally known to me and appears to be of sound mind and acting willingly and free from duress. He or she signed (or asked another to sign for him or her) this document in my presence and that person signed in my presence. I am not the person appointed as agent by this document.

Witnesses ....
Signature   Signature

....
Print name   Print name

....
Address   Address

....

Publisher's Note: This Health Care Proxy is printed on 100% cotton content paper. Unlike ordinary photocopy paper, this quality stock resists turning brittle and brown with age. Insist on genuine Blumberg forms to ensure the longevity of this important document.

The publisher maintains property rights in the layout, graphic design and typestyle of this form as well as in the company's trademarked logo and name. Reproduction of blank copies of this form without the publisher's permission is prohibited. However, once a form has been filled in, photocopying is permitted.

New York State PHL § 2980

Health Care Proxy

....
Date of proxy

....
Person giving proxy

....
Agent

....
Alternate Agent

APPENDIX P:
STATEMENT OF CLIENT'S RIGHTS

The following statement has been approved by the New York State Administrative Board of the Courts to be posted conspicuously in lawyers' offices in New York State beginning January 1, 1998.

Statement of Client's Rights

1. You are entitled to be treated with courtesy and consideration at all times by your lawyer and the other lawyers and personnel in your lawyer's office.

2. You are entitled to an attorney capable of handling your legal matter competently and diligently, in accordance with the highest standards of the profession. If you are not satisfied with how your matter is being handled, you have the right to withdraw from the attorney-client relationship at any time (court approval may be required in some matters, and your attorney may have a claim against you for the value of services rendered to you up to the point of discharge).

3. You are entitled to your lawyer's independent professional judgment and undivided loyalty uncompromised by conflicts of interest.

4. You are entitled to be charged a reasonable fee and to have your lawyer explain at the outset how the fee will be computed and the manner and frequency of billing. You are entitled to request and receive a written itemized bill from your attorney at reasonable intervals. You may refuse to enter into any fee arrangement that you find unsatisfactory.

5. You are entitled to have your questions and concerns addressed in a prompt manner and to have your telephone calls returned promptly.

6. You are entitled to be kept informed as to the status of your matter and to request and receive copies of papers. You are entitled to sufficient

information to allow you to participate meaningfully in the development of your matter.

7. You are entitled to have your legitimate objectives respected by your attorney, including whether or not to settle your matter (court approval of a settlement is required in some matters).

8. You have the right to privacy in dealings with your lawyer and to have your secrets and confidences preserved to the extent permitted by law.

9 You are entitled to have your attorney conduct himself or herself ethically in accordance with the Code of Professional Responsibility.

10. You may not be refused representation on the basis of race, creed, color, religion, sex, sexual orientation, age, national origin, or disability.

APPENDIX Q:

Committee on Professional Ethics, New York State Bar Association, Opinion 610

Opinion 610 - 6/20/90 (2-90)

Topic: Attorney and client; conflicts of interest; wills; executors; beneficiaries.

Digest: Only in limited circumstances may an attorney-draftsman prepare a will in which the attorney-draftsman is named both as executor and as a beneficiary.

Code: DR 5-101(A); EC 5-5, 5-6.

QUESTION

May an attorney draft a client's will naming the attorney as co-executor and also as one of four residuary beneficiaries?

OPINION

The inquiring lawyer wishes to draft a will for an elderly client who was referred to the attorney by another attorney three years ago to provide legal and financial advice for the client's closely held corporation. The inquirer advises that, during the past three years, the client has remained such and has also become a close friend of the inquiring attorney's family. The client's only living relatives are a niece and a nephew with whom the inquirer states the client has very little contact.

The client has requested the inquirer to prepare a will under which the assets of the client's estate will be distributed to her niece, her nephew, her former bookkeeper and various other persons. In addition, the client wishes to appoint her former bookkeeper and the inquiring attorney as co-executors and she wishes the inquirer to be named as one of four residuary beneficiaries. (The residuary estate would consist primarily but not necessarily exclusively of lapsed legacies.) The lawyer inquires whether it is ethically permissible to prepare a will under which the lawyer will receive a bequest and also be named as co-executor.

Lawyer-Draftsman as Beneficiary

Although this Committee has not previously addressed the issue, courts and legislators disfavor bequests to attorney-draftsmen except under extraordinary circumstances. In New York, upon probate, surrogates must investigate any bequest to the attorney who drafted the will. The attorney must submit an affidavit explaining the facts and circumstances of the gift. If the surrogate is not satisfied with the explanation, a hearing is held to determine whether the attorney's bequest was the result of undue influence. *See* N.Y. SCPA § 1408(1) (McKinney 1967). *See generally* Groppe, The "New" Putnam Rule: Problems Facing the Attorney/Legatee/Fiduciary, 61 N.Y.S.B.J. 18 (Jan. 1989); Pace, Problem Areas in Will Drafting Under New York Law, 56 St. John's L. Rev. 459, 473-79 (1982).

This hearing is often referred to as a "Putnam" hearing, so named because of the leading case of *In re Will of Putnam*, 257 N.Y. 140 (1931), in which the New York Court of Appeals suggested that bequests to attorney-draftsmen should be avoided. The *Putnam* court stated that when an attorney-draftsman of a will is a legatee, an inference arises that the attorney used undue influence to secure the bequest. *Id.* at 143. The *Putnam* court therefore advised attorneys to have the will drawn by another attorney if the client intends to leave such a bequest. *Id.*

EC 5-5 of the Code of Professional Responsibility memorializes the *Putnam* rule:

A lawyer should not suggest to his client that a gift be made to himself or for his benefit. If a lawyer accepts a gift from his client, he is peculiarly susceptible to the charge that he unduly influenced or overreached the client. If a client voluntarily offers to make a gift to his lawyer, the lawyer may accept the gift, but before doing so, he should urge that his client secure disinterested advice from an independent, competent person who is cognizant of all the circumstances. Other than in exceptional circumstances, a lawyer should insist that an instrument in which his client desires to name him beneficially be prepared by another lawyer selected by the client.[1]

---

[1] Although the American Bar Associaton's Model Rules of Professional Conduct have not been adopted in New York, it is worth noting that Model Rule 1.8 (c) is stricter than EC 5-5. Unlike EC 5-5, which is merely precatory, Rule 1.8 (c) states that:

A lawyer shall not prepare an instrument giving the lawyer or a person related to the lawyer as parent, child, sibling, or spouse any substantial gift from a client, including a testamentary gift, except where the client is related to that donee. (Emphasis added.)

We believe that the "exceptional circumstances" referred to in EC 5-5 include situations where there is a close familial relationship between the testator and the attorney-draftsman, or where the gift is relatively small in relation to the size of the estate and the professional relationship between the decedent and the attorney-draftsman is longstanding. Although the determination is fact intensive, the Committee does not believe that the situation posed by the inquirer presents the sort of "exceptional circumstances" contemplated by the Code.

This issue has been the subject of several recent New York cases that follow the *Putnam* rule and the Code. *See, e.g., In re Delorey*, 141 A.D.2d 540, 529 N.Y.S.2d 153 (2d Dep't 1988) (court denied probate of a will which named attorney-draftsman as sole legatee); *In re Tank*, 132 Misc. 2d 146, 503 N.Y.S.2d 495 (Sup. Ct. 1986) (court held that attorney-draftsman's acceptance of a $5,000 bequest involved overreaching and a breach of professional responsibility to the testatrix); *In re Estate of Cromwell*, No. 2241-P-1986 (Sur. Ct. Suffolk County, Jan. 27, 1989) (LEXIS, States library, NY File) ($500,000 legacy to attorney-draftsman and appointment of attorney-draftsman's partner as co-executor upheld where record established a "longstanding professional relationship" as well as close personal family ties, but court ordered law firm to pay costs of hearing); *Estate of Arnold*, 125 Misc. 2d 265, 479 N.Y.S.2d 924 (Sur. Ct. 1983) ($2,000 bequest to wife of attorney-draftsman upheld as product of friendly social relationship which had endured for several years); *In re Annesley*, 97 Misc. 2d 1047, 412 N.Y.S.2d 959 (Sur. Ct. 1979) (bequest of small fraction of estate to attorney-draftsman nephew who maintained very close relationship with aunt upheld).

These cases indicate that even though a bequest to an attorney-draftsman may ultimately be upheld upon a strong evidentiary showing, the so-called *Putnam* hearing can delay and increase the expense of probate to the prejudice of other parties to the will. The attorney-draftsman has an obligation to advise the client of this fact and of all other relevant considerations. If, after being fully informed of these matters, the client nevertheless insists that the lawyer draft the instrument naming the lawyer beneficially, and if the "exceptional circumstances" referred to in EC 5-5 are present, it would not be unethical for the lawyer to draft the will. In that situation, the client's wishes and the fact that the client has been advised of the relevant considerations should be documented.

Lawyer-Draftsman as Co-Executor

In the question presented, the lawyer-draftsman who will receive the bequest under the will also proposes to serve as co-executor of the estate. This issue is specifically addressed by EC 5-6 of the Code of Professional Responsibility:

APPENDIX R:
The Estate Project for Artists with AIDS

APPENDIX R:
THE ESTATE PROJECT FOR ARTISTS WITH AIDS
Patrick Moore, Director

Project Background

In 1991, the Alliance for the Arts initiated the Estate Project for Artists with AIDS as a research project to develop useful advice for artists on estate planning and strategic direction for the arts community in the face of the enormous cultural losses created by AIDS. Artists with HIV/AIDS faced particularly complex issues, especially those who were gay or lesbian. Future Safe was intended to explain, in easily understood terms, the basic issues of estate planning for artists. Future Safe's basic premise is that the artist must become motivated to help himself and then turn to legal counsel once certain decisions had been made.

The Estate Project worked closely, and supported financially, a range of programs in New York to provide a network of services. Of particular interest is Volunteer Lawyers for the Arts (VLA). VLA's Artist Legacy Project used Future Safe and other specially developed materials to counsel artists and make legal provisions for them, including wills.

The Estate Project has also supported the work of Visual AIDS and developed several collaborative projects with the organization. Visual AIDS is most well known for developing the Red Ribbon. However, the organization now provides a range of services to artists living with HIV disease through its Archive Project. The Archive Project documents the work of artists living with HIV and unable to arrange for the often expensive process of professional documentation. These slides form much of the content in the Estate Project's Virtual Collection, described below.

By 1993, the Estate Project's work had been featured on the front page of the New York Times and the project was actively pursuing a national program of archival projects. At this point, the project is fully operational in New York, Los Angeles, and Miami with active working relationships with institutions ranging from the New York Public Library to the Getty Information Institute and the Solomon R. Guggenheim Museum.

The Estate Project currently has three main, national programs in addition to its publications:

The Virtual Collection is a digital archive of work by visual artists with AIDS that has been developed in conjunction with the Getty Information Institute. The Virtual Collection brings together a huge collection of images created by artists with AIDS and, by using sophisticated technology, makes it possible for curators and historians to access this material without sorting through thousands of fragile slides. The Virtual Collection will be accessible through leading libraries and museums, as well as the Internet. The Estate Project's redesigned website located at http://www.artistswithaids.org will feature both the Virtual Collection and on-line versions of Future Safe and other publications.

An even larger effort is the Estate Project's initiative to catalog and preserve the majority of **AIDS activist videos** made in America. We believe these fragile records will form an invaluable resource in later studying and presenting this moment in history. A core group of important tapes has already been preserved and housed at the New York Public Library. We intend to nationalize this effort and preserve 1,000 hours of tape.

Finally, on September 30, 1997, the Estate Project's first *film preservation* effort had its world premiere at the New York Film Festival. This first film, *Whiplash,* by the well-respected experimental filmmaker Warren Sonbert, has been used as a pilot project to develop standards of preservation. The Estate Project's film preservation project has been undertaken in partnership with the Academy of Motion Picture Arts & Sciences and the Guggenheim Museum. The Estate Project has also begun work on the estate of Jack Smith.

The Estate Project views the art works created by artists with HIV/AIDS crisis as vital historical records of a time of crisis. Comprehensive records such as these, stored in top-level archives, will be a treasure trove for historians hundreds of years from now. We believe much can be learned by the process of completing these projects and teaching other communities what we have learned.

An Anecdote

There has always been much made of the fact that most of the artists involved in the Estate Project's work have not achieved commercial success, as if that relegated them to a status where they were not worthy of basic services such as documentation and wills. It is interesting to look at two mid-career artists whose work has been somewhat hampered by the fact that proper estate planning was not done before their deaths.

Jimmy de Sana and Mark Morrisroe were both well-regarded photographers, producing challenging work that was recognized in the commercial world. It might be assumed that their work would thrive posthumously, nurtured by art world friends and a committed, intelligent dealer (Pat Hearn).

However, both de Sana and Morrisroe left a mass of uncatalogued negatives and source material. Not only were these materials an unworkable burden for Hearn and others entrusted with the arts, they were in a fundamental way only truly understandable to the artists themselves. While informed archivists might conjecture which images were to be printed and in what way, only the artists could have made their wishes known accurately.

Finally, several years later, Hearn has been awarded a grant from the Robert D. Farber Foundation to support the extensive work needed to fully catalog the estates. Although there is much interest in the work of both artists, including museum shows, only now will the work begin to be fully utilized.

Numerous examples of this type exist, ranging the gamut from famous artists such as Keith Haring to unknown artists who have never been shown. The leveling factor in all cases is that only informed decisions by the artists, while they are still well, make for an effective plan.

Conclusion

AIDS has had the effect of bringing to the fore issues that have long been unresolved in American culture. Much as AIDS has focused attention on the fact that our country's health care system is fundamentally flawed, it has also pointed out that our cultural legacy is rather fragile. It is the Estate Project's view that there is an incentive for both the individual and the arts community to value the process of making plans to safeguard the cultural records that will later illustrate this time of crisis.

APPENDIX S:
Resource Directory: Organizations and Publications

APPENDIX S:
RESOURCE DIRECTORY: ORGANI-
ZATIONS AND PUBLICATIONS

Organizations:

Americans for the Arts
927 15th Street, NW 12th Floor
Washington, DC 20005
(202) 371-2830

Choice in Dying
475 Riverside Drive, Room 1852
New York, NY 10115
(212) 870-2003
1-800-989-9455

The Estate Project for Artists with
AIDS
The Alliance for the Arts
330 West 42nd Street
New York, NY 10036
(212) 947-6340
(212) 947-6416 (fax)

New York Foundation for the Arts
155 Avenue of the Americas,
14th Floor
New York, NY 10013
(212) 366-6900

New York Public Library
5th Avenue & 42nd Street
New York, NY 10018
(212) 930-0566

Visual AIDS
526 West 26th Street #510
New York, NY 10001
(212) 627-9855

Visual Artist Information Hotline
Operating Hours are
Monday–Friday,
2:00-5:00 p.m. Eastern Time
1-800-232-2789

Archives of American Art
Smithsonian Institution
8th & G Streets, NW
Washington, DC 20560
(202) 357-2781
(202) 786-2608 (fax)

Archives of American Art
Branches

Boston:
87 Mount Vernon Street
Boston, MA 02108
(617) 565-8444
(617) 565-8466 (fax)

California:
Huntington Library
1151 Oxford Road
San Marino, CA 91108
(818) 583-7847
(818) 583-7207 (fax)

Detroit:
5200 Woodward Avenue
Detroit, MI 48202
(313) 226-7544
(313) 226-7620 (fax)

New York Regional Center:
1285 Avenue of the Americas, 2nd
Floor
New York, NY 10019
(212) 399-5015
(212) 399-6890 (fax)

**A Partial Listing of Volunteer
Lawyers for the Arts:**

Volunteer Lawyers for the Arts,
NYC
1 East 53rd Street, 6th Floor
New York, NY 10022
(212) 319-2787

California Lawyers for the Arts
Santa Monica:
1641 18th Street
Santa Monica, CA 90404
(310) 998-5590

San Francisco:
Fort Mason Center
Building C, Room 255
San Francisco, CA 94123
(415) 775-7200

Washington Area Lawyers for the
Arts
815 15th Street NW, Suite 900
Washington, DC 20005
(202) 393-2826

Lawyers for the Creative Arts
213 West Institute Place, Suite 411
Chicago, IL 60610-3125
(312) 944-ARTS

Mid-America Arts Resources
P.O. Box 363
Lindsborg, KS 67456
(913) 227-2321

Philadelphia Volunteer Lawyers for
the Arts
251 South 18th Street
Philadelphia, PA 19103
(215) 545-3385

Texas Accountants and Lawyers
for the Arts
2917 Swiss Avenue
Dallas, TX 75204
(214) 821-1818

Artists Legal and Accounting
Assistance
P.O. Box 2577
Austin, TX 78768
(512) 476-4458

Texas Accountants and Lawyers for the Arts
1540 Sul Ross
Houston, TX 77006
(713) 526-4876

Volunteer Lawyers for the Arts/ Florida ArtServe, Inc.
1350 East Sunrise Boulevard, Suite 100
Ft. Lauderdale, FL 33304
(954) 462-9191

For Volunteer Lawyers for the Arts in states not listed call the New York office
(212) 319-2787

Publications:

Alliance for the Arts. *The Report of the Estate Project for Artists with AIDS*. 1992.

Americans for the Arts 1998 Publications Catalogue.

Association of the Bar of the City of New York, "You Can't Take It With You: Estate Planning and Administration for the Visual Artist," December 15, 1997. Audio tape available from the Association, $25.00 members, $35 nonmembers. Call (212) 382-6654.

Bell, Douglas J. *Changing I.R.C. @ 170(e)(1)(A): For Art's Sake*. 1987. Case Western Reserve Law Review, Case Western Reserve University.

Bridges, F. *Portrait of the Artist as a Limited Partner*. 21 Tax Mgmt. Est., Gifts and Tr. J. 83 (March/April 1996).

Clifford, Denis and Cora Jordan. *Plan Your Estate*. NOLO Press, 1996. To order, please contact VLA/NYC (212) 319-2787.

Crawford, Tad. *Legal Guide for the Visual Artist, The Professional's Handbook, Revised 3rd Expanded Edition*. Allworth Press, 1995.

Fraiman, Genevieve L. and Jennifer B. Jordan. *The Management Portfolio: T.M. 815, Estate Planning for Authors and Artists*. 1998.

Future Safe. A Publication of the Estate Project for Artists with AIDS. Alliance for the Arts, 1997.

Hoot, Scott, editor. *Estate Planning for Artists: Will Your Art Survive?* A Symposium Sponsored by Volunteer Lawyers for the Arts. 21 Columbia VLA J.L. & Arts 15 (1996).
For copies, call (212) 854-1607.

Lerner, R. and J. Bresler. *ART LAW, The Guide for Collectors, Investors, Dealers and Artists,* 2nd Ed., (P.L.I., 1997), Vol. 2.

Note: *Federal Estate Tax and the Right of Publicity: Taxing Estates for Celebrity Value,* 108 Harvard Law Review 683 (Jan. 1995).

Perotta, D. *Estate Planning for Owners of Patents and Copyrights,* 21 Est. Plan. 94, 95-96 (1994).

Schaengold, D. *Valuation of Artists' Estates: David Smith, Georgia O' Keeffe and Andy Warhol—Have We Missed the Forest for the Trees?* 20 Tax Mgmt. Est., Gifts & Tr. J. 167, (Nov./Dec. 1995).

Texas Accountants and Lawyers for the Arts, Artist Estate Planning Project. *Basic Considerations in Estate Planning with an Emphasis in Representing the Artist.* 1996.

APPENDIX T:

Visual Artists Estate Planning Conference Participants

APPENDIX T:
VISUAL ARTISTS ESTATE PLANNING CONFERENCE PARTICIPANTS

Facilitators

Chuck Close
Artist
Artists Advisory Committee
The Marie Walsh Sharpe Art
Foundation

Irving Sandler
Professor of Art History
SUNY Purchase
Artists Advisory Committee
The Marie Walsh Sharpe Art
Foundation

Robert Storr
Curator, Department of Painting &
Sculpture
The Museum of Modern Art
Artists Advisory Committee
The Marie Walsh Sharpe Art
Foundation

Participants

Roger Anthony
Collections Manager
The DeKooning Conservatorship

Charles Bergman
Executive Vice President
The Pollock-Krasner Foundation

Avis Berman
Writer and Art Historian

David Brown, Esq.
Cooper, Brown & Behrle, P.C.

Cynthia Carlson
Artist
Artists Advisory Committee
The Marie Walsh Sharpe Art
Foundation

Elizabeth Catlett
Artist

Betty Cuningham
Associate Director
Hirschl & Adler Modern

Gilbert S. Edelson, Esq.
Rosenman & Colin
Administrative Vice President
Art Dealers Association of America

Andre Emmerich
Andre Emmerich—A Division of
Sotheby's

Janet Fish
Artist
Artists Advisory Committee
The Marie Walsh Sharpe Art
Foundation

Stephen E. Weil, Esq.
Emeritus Senior Scholar
Center for Museum Studies
Smithsonian Institution

Beverly Wolff, Esq.
General Counsel
The Museum of Modern Art

Betty Woodman
Artist

Observers

William Feltzin
Accountant

John Oddy
Vice President, Grant Program
The Judith Rothschild Foundation

William Pearlstein, Esq.
Golenbock, Eiseman, Assor, & Bell

Representing The Marie Walsh
Sharpe Art Foundation

Joyce E. Robinson
Vice President/Executive Director

Kim M. Taylor
Administrative Assistant

Andy Tirado
Assistant

APPENDIX U:

Members of the Committee on Art Law

APPENDIX U:
MEMBERS OF THE COMMITTEE ON ART LAW

* Barbara T. Hoffman, Esq., Chair

Herbert Hirsch, Esq., Secretary

Sallie Ballantine, Esq.

* Christina M. Baltz, Esq.

Patrick Walter Begos, Esq.

William M. Borchard, Esq.

Susan D. Brown, Esq.

Judith Lynn Church, Esq.

Bara Diokhane, Esq.

Gilbert S. Edelson, Esq.

Jeremy G. Epstein, Esq.

* Genevieve L. Fraiman, Esq.

Lee White Galvis, Esq.

Peter P. McN. Gates, Esq.

Philomene A. Gates, Esq.

Ashton Hawkins, Esq.

Theodore N. Kaplan, Esq.

Roy S. Kaufman, Esq.

Pamela A. Mann, Esq.

Slade R. Metcalf, Esq.

Millard L. Midonick, Esq.

Rena J. Moulopoulos, Esq.

Herbert E. Nass, Esq.

William G. Pearlstein, Esq.

Maxine S. Pfeffer, Esq.

Michael D. Rips, Esq.

John Sare, Esq.

Selvyn Seidel, Esq.

Ronald D. Spencer, Esq.

* Erik J. Stapper, Esq.

Michael Ward Stout, Esq.

Daniel H. Weiner, Esq.

Louise E. Weiss, Esq.

Carl L. Zanger, Esq.

David S. Brown, Esq., Adjunct

Susan M. Brown, Intern

* Members of the Publication Committee for the *A Visual Artist's Guide to Estate Planning* book

FOUNDATION INFORMATION

THE MARIE WALSH SHARPE ART FOUNDATION

711 North Tejon Street, Suite B
Colorado Springs, CO 80903
(719) 635-3220

President
Charles J. Hemmingsen

Vice President and Executive Director
Joyce E. Robinson

Administrative Assistant
Kimberly M. Taylor

Program Associate
Nanette L. Tirado

THE JUDITH ROTHSCHILD FOUNDATION

1110 Park Avenue
New York, NY 10128
(212) 831-4114

Trustee
Harvey S. Shipley Miller

Vice President, Grant Program
John James Oddy